W9-BZC-443

A PASSAGE TO INDIA

Nation and Narration

TWAYNE'S MASTERWORK STUDIES

Robert Lecker, General Editor

A PASSAGE TO INDIA

Nation and Narration

Judith Scherer Herz

TWAYNE PUBLISHERS ♦ NEW YORK

Maxwell Macmillan Canada ♦ Toronto

Maxwell Macmillan International ♦ New York   Oxford   Singapore   Sydney

Twayne's Masterwork Studies No. 117

Copyright © 1993 by Twayne Publishers

All rights reserved. No part of this book may be reproduced or transmitted in any form or by any means, electronic or mechanical, including photocopying, recording, or by any information storage and retrieval system, without permission in writing from the Publisher.

Twayne Publishers
Macmillan Publishing Company
866 Third Avenue
New York, New York 10022

Maxwell Macmillan Canada, Inc.
1200 Eglinton Avenue East
Suite 200
Don Mills, Ontario M3C 3N1

Macmillan Publishing Company is a part of the Maxwell Communication Group of Companies.

Library of Congress Cataloging-in-Publication Data

Herz, Judith Scherer
A passage to India : nation and narration / Judith Scherer Herz.
p.   cm. — (Twayne's masterwork studies ; no. 117)
Includes bibliographical references and index.
ISBN 0-8057-8056-4. — ISBN 0-8057-8104-8 (pbk.)
1. Forster, E. M. (Edward Morgan), 1879–1970. Passage to India. 2. India in literature.   I. Title. II. Series.
PR6011.058P3744   1993

823'.912—dc20   92-30294
                                                      CIP

The paper used in this publication meets the minimum requirements of American National Standard for Information Sciences—Permanence of Paper for Printed Library Materials, ANSI Z39.48-1984.

10 9 8 7 6 5 4 3 2 1 (alk. paper)

10 9 8 7 6 5 4 3 2 1 (pbk.: alk. paper)

Printed in the United States of America.

For Rachel, Nathaniel, and Carl

Contents

Acknowledgments   ix

Chronology: E. M. Forster's Life and Works   xi

LITERARY AND HISTORICAL CONTEXT

1. A Modernist Novel?   3
2. The British Raj and the Writing of *A Passage to India*   11
3. "Expansion . . . Not Completion"   31
4. Critical Reception   35

A READING

5. World and Text   45
6. Beginnings   61
7. Narration and Language   73
8. Caves   91
9. Trials   103
10. Endings   113
11. Epilogue: Ghosts and Memory   127

Notes   135
Bibliography   143
Index   147

Acknowledgments

A much earlier version of some of the material in chapters 7, 8, and 10 originally appeared in "Listening to Language," in *A Passage to India: Essays in Interpretation*, edited by John Beer (London: Macmillan Press, 1985).

I wish to thank the Society of Authors as the Literary Representatives of the Estate of E. M. Forster, the Provost and Scholars of King's College, Cambridge, the Henry W. and Albert A. Berg Collection, the New York Public Library, and the Astor, Lenox, and Tilden Foundations for permission to quote from unpublished material, and the National Portrait Gallery (London) for permission to reproduce the photograph of E. M. Forster by Howard Coster.

My thanks, too, to the students of a terrific Forster seminar a few years back, especially to Michèle Richman; to my colleague Robert Martin for advice, encouragement, and many patient readings; to my son, Nathaniel, who read the manuscript with scrupulous attention and understanding, and who helped in countless ways; and to Rachel and Carl and my other loving friends and relations.

E. M. Forster, 1938. Photo by Howard Coster. From the National Portrait Gallery, London.

Chronology:
E. M. Forster's Life and Works

1879	Edward Morgan Forster born 1 January to Edward Morgan Llewellyn Forster and Alice Clara (Lily) Whichelo.
1880	Father dies of tuberculosis.
1883	Mother moves with Forster to Rooksnest, the house that becomes the model for *Howards End*.
1887	Death of great-aunt, Marianne Thornton, a figure in the Clapham sect (bankers, philanthropists, abolitionists); she leaves Forster bequest of £8,000 and thus provides for his later education and travel.
1890	Attends Kent House School.
1893	Day boy at Tonbridge School (provides scenes for Sawston in *The Longest Journey*).
1897	Enters King's College, Cambridge; studies classics.
1900	First published writing appears in *Cambridge Review* and in *Basileona*. Takes upper second class in Classical Tripos; receives B.A.
1901	Stays at Cambridge for fourth year to read history; begins work on a novel, *Nottingham Lace* (never completed); elected to the Cambridge Conversazione Society (the Apostles), a secret undergraduate debating society, founded 1820, whose members included G. E. Moore, Roger Fry, Bertrand Russell, and John Maynard Keynes. Begins a year's travels in

	Italy and Austria; this trip and a subsequent one in 1903 to Italy and Greece will influence much of his early fiction as well as his historical essays.
1902	Begins work on a novel that will eventually become *A Room with a View*; gives Latin classes at the Working Men's College (London); will continue lecturing there for the next 20 years.
1903	First story, "Albergo Empedocle," published in *Temple Bar*; begins publishing essays and stories in the the newly founded *Independent Review*.
1905	Goes to Germany to tutor to the children of the Countess von Arnim (author of *Elizabeth and Her German Garden*, 1898); publishes *Where Angels Fear to Tread*.
1906	Publication of E. Fairfax Taylor's translation of the *Aeneid, with Introduction and Notes by EMF*; becomes Latin tutor to Syed Ross Masood, to whom *A Passage to India* is dedicated.
1907	Publishes *The Longest Journey*.
1908	Publishes *A Room with a View*; begins reading the *Koran*.
1910	Publishes *Howards End*; begins wide-ranging reading in Indian history, politics, art, and religion.
1911	Publishes *The Celestial Omnibus*; begins working on *Arctic Summer* (unfinished).
1912	In preparation for trip to India, learns some Urdu, rereads the Bhagavad Gita, takes riding lessons. Leaves with R. Trevelyan and G. L. Dickinson; visits Masood and travels extensively, including visits to the Native States of Chhatarpur and Dewas.
1913	Returns from India in April; begins working on *A Passage to India*; visits Edward Carpenter, author of *The Intermediate Sex* (1908) about the "Uranian," or homosexual, temperament; the encounter prompts Forster to start writing *Maurice*.

1914   Finishes *Maurice*, which remains unpublished until after Forster's death; works as cataloger at the National Gallery; plans to write a book about Samuel Butler (project abandoned the following year). In August, Britain declares war on Germany.

1915   Begins friendship with D. H. Lawrence; goes to Alexandria as searcher for the Red Cross (November 1915 to January 1919).

1916   Meets the Greek poet C. P. Cavafy, whose poetry Forster later arranges to have translated and published in England.

1917   Begins relationship with Mohammed el Adl; publishes articles in the *Egyptian Mail* (continues through 1918).

1918   First World War ends 11 November; returns to Britain in early 1919 and writes for several newspapers and magazines.

1920   Becomes temporary literary editor of the *Daily Herald*; publishes *The Story of the Siren* as Hogarth Press pamphlet; publication of *The Government of Egypt, with Notes on Egypt by EMF*.

1921   Begins attending meetings of Memoir Club (Bloomsbury); takes second trip to India: visits Masood; goes to Dewas as private secretary to the Maharajah; attempts unsuccessfully to continue his India novel.

1922   On return from India, stops at Mansourah to see el Adl, now dying of tuberculosis. In Britain, publishes essays on India and returns to work on *A Passage to India* after burning many of his erotic stories (although he saves some and continues to write others, notably "The Life to Come"); publishes *Alexandria: A History and a Guide*. Begins friendship with J. R. Ackerley.

1923   Publishes *Pharos and Pharillon*.

1924	Publication on 4 June of *A Passage to India*; his aunt Laura dies, leaving him the leasehold of her West Hackhurst house in Abinger Hammer, to which he and his mother move; *The Celestial Omnibus* published in United States.
1925	Publication of *Eliza Fay's Original Letters from India (1779–1815), with Introduction and Terminal Notes by EMF*; *A Passage to India* is awarded the James Tait Black Prize and the Femina–Vie Heureuse Prize; begins writing in his *Commonplace Book*.
1927	Delivers Clark Lectures at Trinity College, Cambridge; published as *Aspects of the Novel*.
1928	Publishes *"The Eternal Moment" and Other Stories*; with Virginia Woolf, protests the censoring of Radclyffe Hall's *The Well of Loneliness*.
1929	Travels to Africa.
1930	Meets Bob Buckingham, beginning of intimate friendship that lasts until Forster's death.
1931	Delivers lecture, "The Creator as Critic," to the Cambridge English faculty; publishes *A Letter to Madan Blanchard* in the Hogarth Press Letters Series.
1932	Begins series of broadcasts on books for the BBC (he had begun broadcasting in 1928 and would continue for the next 30 years, giving some 145 broadcasts); Bob Buckingham marries; his friend Goldsworthy Lowes Dickinson (writer, Cambridge figure active in the founding of the League of Nations) dies; Forster begins work on Dickinson's biography; begins friendship with Christopher Isherwood.
1934	Publishes *Goldsworthy Lowes Dickinson*; becomes first president of the newly founded National Council for Civil Liberties; writes *Pageant of Abinger* (with music by Ralph Vaughan Williams).
1935	Mulk Raj Anand's *Untouchable: A Novel* is published with preface by Forster; speaks on "Liberty in England" at the International Writers' Congress in Paris.

1936	Publishes *Abinger Harvest* (a collection of his essays).
1937	Syed Ross Masood and the Maharajah of Dewas die.
1938	Writes *England's Pleasant Land* (with music by Ralph Vaughan Williams); first publication of essay, "Two Cheers for Democracy," revised as "Credo" and then republished as "What I Believe"; Neville Chamberlain, British prime minister, signs Munich Pact with Germany, claiming to have secured "peace in our time."
1939	3 September, Britain declares war on Germany immediately following Germany's invasion of Poland.
1940	Publishes *Nordic Twilight* in the Macmillan War Pamphlet Series; is instrumental in the publication of Ahmed Ali's first novel, *Twilight in Delhi.*
1941	Suicide of Virginia Woolf on 28 March. Delivers Rede Lecture in Cambridge on her work (published in 1942); begins broadcasting to India in the series *Some Books* on BBC Overseas Service (renamed Eastern Service in 1942).
1944	Delivers the W. P. Ker Memorial Lecture at the University of Glasgow, "The Development of English Prose."
1945	Death of his mother; end of war in Europe on 7 May; third visit to India to attend the All India Writers' Conference in Jaipur.
1946	Leaves West Hackhurst for Cambridge; elected Honorary Fellow of King's College; has study in college and lodgings in town.
1947	Visits United States to deliver lecture, "The Raison d'Etre of Criticism in the Arts," at Harvard University Symposium on Music Criticism; publication in the United States of *The Collected Tales of E. M. Forster* (called *The Collected Short Stories* when published in Britain the following year); receives honorary doctorate from the University of Liverpool.

1949	Second visit to the United States; delivers lecture, "Art for Art's Sake," to the American Academy and National Institute of Arts and Letters; receives honorary doctorate from Hamilton College.
1950	Receives honorary doctorate from Cambridge University and, in the following year, from University of Nottingham.
1951	Publication of *Two Cheers for Democracy* (a collection of his essays); premiere of *Billy Budd*, libretto by Forster and Eric Crozier, music by Benjamin Britten, published the following year.
1953	Receives the Companion of Honour from the Queen; publication of *The Hill of Devi*; moves into King's College.
1954	Receives honorary doctorates from the University of Manchester and Leiden University.
1956	Publishes *Marianne Thornton*, a biography of his great-aunt.
1958	Receives honorary doctorate from the University of Leicester.
1959	Gives the Presidential Address to the Cambridge Humanists.
1960	Adds a "Terminal Note" to *Maurice* (the novel remained unpublished); is a witness for the defense in the obscenity trial of Lawrence's *Lady Chatterley's Lover*.
1961	Is inducted into the Royal Society of Literature as Companion of Literature; publishes his last review, which is of Leonard Woolf's *Growing: An Autobiography of the Years 1904–1911*.
1962	Writes introduction to Golding's *Lord of the Flies*.
1963	Publishes short story, "Arctic Summer: Fragment of an Unfinished Novel."
1964	Suffers slight stroke.
1969	Receives the Order of Merit.

1970   Dies on 7 June in the Coventry home of Bob and May Buckingham.

1971   Publication of *Maurice* and of *"Albergo Empedocle" and Other Writings*.

1972   Publication of *"The Life to Come" and Other Stories*.

1978   Publication of the *Commonplace Book*.

1980   Publication of *Arctic Summer and Other Fiction*.

LITERARY AND
HISTORICAL CONTEXT

1

A Modernist Novel?

Between 1905 and 1910 four of the five novels that Forster published in his lifetime appeared. When the fifth, *A Passage to India*, was published in 1924 it was treated as a major literary event. The comment that opened John Middleton Murry's review was typical: "It was only to be expected that E. M. Forster's novel when it did come, after a silence of fourteen years, would be a remarkable one."[1] Forster had certainly not been forgotten during that interval; still, many wondered at the silence, given the extraordinary creative burst that had marked the start of his career. He did remain in public view, however, frequently publishing essays and reviews. At the end of the decade he gathered some of the journalism he had written while in Egypt during the First World War in *Pharos and Pharillon* (1922), and in 1923 he published *Alexandria: A History and a Guide*.

He continued to write fiction throughout this period, but he had little to show for it. Early in the decade, he had begun a novel set in India, but he had not made much progress and had abandoned it along with the beginning of another unfinished novel, *Arctic Summer*, a fragment that finally yielded, many years later, the posthumously published story called "The Other Boat." The novel that he did finish, *Maurice*, a homosexual love story with an emphatically happy ending,[2] could not have been published easily in 1914 and remained in manuscript until after his death, along with several short stories that he also wrote during this period, including the remarkable "The Life to Come." Forster's not being able to acknowledge publicly the writing that most absorbed him

3

and not being certain what direction to follow after his early success are the most likely explanations for the much-remarked 14-year silence.

Furthermore, although he had been hailed in 1910 as "one of the great novelists" (Gardner, 130) and pronounced important and remarkable, there was very little consensus as to the nature of that greatness. He was seen as an original; as an anonymous reviewer observed, his writing "occupies a niche entirely by itself. . . . It is not like anything else that is being done" (Gardner, 128). Or, as another reviewer asserted, "there is no novelist living on whom one can more confidently rely for unexpected developments" (Gardner, 132). And in 1924, before the publication of *A Passage to India*, in a review that went back to *Howards End* and *The Celestial Omnibus* as a way of elucidating the qualities of *Pharos and Pharillon*, he was described as "urbanely, tranquilly, unmistakably unique" (Gardner, 191).

Unique and elusive (another favorite adjective), someone of whom great things were expected, he nonetheless elicited considerable puzzlement as well as praise on the part of reviewers and critics who tried to place him in the English literary tradition. Linked to George Meredith, Henry James, and Joseph Conrad, he was also frequently compared to Arnold Bennett and John Galsworthy. He seemed to be working in the realist tradition of the English novel and for the most part in the comic, ironic mode presided over by Meredith's comic muse, who is explicitly invoked in *A Room with a View*. Thackeray and Trollope were also audible presences in his early fiction, as was most certainly Austen. But reviewers heard other voices in his fictional rooms and could not quite describe the resulting sound. For his social realism cohabited with the fantastic and the poetic, especially in the short stories where gods and fauns mingled among the well-brought-up English. It is a narrative mode best described by the novelist Elizabeth Bowen, herself very much under Forster's influence in this regard, as "the welding of the inexplicable and the banal."[3]

He was not quite like any of his predecessors, nor like his contemporaries, although he was certainly closer to James and Conrad than to those whom Virginia Woolf in a 1919 essay called "the materialists." She was referring to Bennett, Galsworthy, Wells—writers who took "too much delight in the solidity of [their] fabric,"[4] crafters of well-made books set in equally well-upholstered houses. Like James and Conrad, however, Forster was directly concerned with the representation of subjectivity within a social world marked by flux and uncertainty. As Michael Levenson describes this concern in a recent study, particularly in reference to *Howards End,* "Conrad, James and Forster each attempt to draw a circle of individuality within the wreck of social life, and then each attempts to move from the naked ego towards a reinvented community. . . . [E]ach represents a cautious attempt, fraught with uncertainty, to extend intimacy, to transmit perception, to share meanings and in this way to restore a possible basis for social life."[5] But James had died in 1916, his last novel having been published in 1905, and while Conrad's reputation was still considerable in the early 1920s, his most important fiction had been written 10 to 20 years earlier. Although both Galsworthy and Bennett remained popular, they were entirely apart from the literary vanguard. Galsworthy's *The Forsyte Saga,* bringing together three novels published in 1906, 1920, and 1921, was published in 1922. But that Victorian vestige appeared in the same year as T. S. Eliot's *The Waste Land,* James Joyce's *Ulysses,* Virginia Woolf's *Jacob's Room,* and D. H. Lawrence's *Aaron's Rod.* Lytton Strachey's *Queen Victoria* was published the year before, and Ezra Pound's *Hugh Selwyn Mauberley,* two years earlier. This was the very height of the modernist movement in British letters—or, indeed, in Western art altogether, if we add Proust, Gide, Stein, Mann, Picasso, Chagall, Stravinsky, and Diaghilev (among numerous other possibilities) to the list.

It is an open question whether Forster's name belongs on this list. Had he not written *A Passage to India,* the consensus no doubt would be "probably not." At the same time, like his more avant-garde contemporaries, he was "bored . . . by the tiresomeness and conventionalities of fiction form."[6] Yet the breakup of these conventions in the work of Joyce and Woolf that appeared during the period of his writing *A Passage to India* held little interest for him. His essentially nineteenth-century belief that characters should "live continuously"—that is, like Tolstoy's, continue beyond the book[7]—prevented him from moving in Woolf's direction. Of course, Woolf's major work was yet to come, and Forster was a strong supporter of her "wonderful new method" (*AH,* 114), but it was not a method for him. Thus, in the early 1920s when Forster returned to working on his India novel, he faced a loss of confidence both in his own abilities and in the fictional forms available to him. Moreover, as he discovered in his second visit to India in 1921, British rule no longer seemed stable and permanent. The world he had begun writing about a decade earlier had changed utterly.

Unlike the more committed modernists, Forster did not share the assumption of the autonomy of the object of art, although he did believe in its anonymity and essential impersonality. For the modernist, art no longer meant imitating—that is, replicating, or pretending to replicate—reality, but instead finding a new reality altogether. Thus the modernist novelist, in David Lodge's formulation, discovered "that the effort to capture reality in narrative fiction, pursued with a certain degree of intensity, brings the writer out on the other side of realism."[8] This is what Woolf meant in the 1919 essay already cited when she enjoined her contemporaries to "record the atoms as they fall upon the mind in the order in which they fall[;] let us trace the pattern, however disconnected and incoherent in appearance, which each sight or incident scores upon the consciousness" (Woolf, 2:106). In a diary entry she made the reason for this task even clearer: "The method of writing smooth narrative cant be right; things don't happen in one's mind like that."[9] Forster did not write "smooth narrative" in Woolf's pejorative sense, but neither did he record the atoms as they fell.

The two writers among her contemporaries whom Woolf saw as sharing something of her vision of the novel were Forster and D. H. Lawrence, both of whom were working in a similar symbolist-realist mode. However, neither of them in her view followed this new way of seeing with sufficient single-mindedness. "Mr. Forster and Mr. Lawrence . . . spoilt their early work because . . . they tried to compromise. They tried to combine their own direct sense of the oddity and significance of some character with Mr. Galsworthy's knowledge of the Factory Acts, and Mr. Bennett's knowledge of the Five Towns" (Woolf, 1:333).

All three writers shared the modernist interest in the nature of subjectivity and in the construction of gender. However, from our vantage, Forster's writing probably stands in a more interesting relationship to Woolf's (especially to her fiction of the mid- to late 1920s—*Mrs. Dalloway, To the Lighthouse, Orlando*) than to

Lawrence's, precisely because both Forster and Woolf were more critical of the modernist myth of origins than was Lawrence.[10] Forster, in particular, was deeply uneasy with the idea that one could return to some privileged and purified originating moment even though his own writing was suffused with a nostalgia, often ironically presented, for the past. Forster was clearly attracted to Lawrence's reverence for the instinctual, but he was very wary of the potential dangers of such beliefs, for he was much more of a rationalist and an intellectual. Lawrence, by contrast, was a profoundly mythic writer, "a sandy haired passionate Nibelung" (Lago and Furbank, 1:217) in Forster's description after their first meeting in 1915, who had few of Forster's reticences and reservations. Their very different fictional worlds share neither linguistic registers nor range of cultural allusions, but they are built on a similar antithesis between nature and civilization, even if their creators would probably not have agreed on the significance of either term. Despite their uneasy friendship in which each was essentially disappointed in the other, there was still considerable respect for the other's work, especially on Forster's part. It is worth noting that Forster's angry letter to the *Nation and Athenaeum* (29 March 1930), partly in response to the belittling obituary for Lawrence in the *Times*, is unequivocal in its claim that "he was the greatest imaginative novelist of our generation."[11]

The word "modernism" appears frequently in the literary history of this period, but its terms of reference are hard to pin down. Should the emphasis be on formal matters or epistemological issues—that is, attitudes toward history and human reason? If the art of any age always reacts against or resists the conventions and assumptions of the former, what was so particular about the process of change in the second and third decades of this century? What sense can we make of Virginia Woolf's comment in a lecture she gave in 1924—"in or about December, 1910, human character changed" (Woolf, 1:320)? She may have had any number of specific events in mind (or none)—the first postimpressionist show, organized by her friend Roger Fry, or the death of Tolstoy, or the death of Edward VII, or the labor unrest that began in the coal mines in 1910 and spread to the London docks the following year. There is certainly perceivable change around that date, even though aspects of what we call modernism can be traced to the late nineteenth century, especially to Samuel Butler and to the aesthetic tradition of Pater and Wilde. As well, the term functions as an umbrella for a variety of schools, movements, groups, and ideologies. Vorticism, cubism, imagism, postimpressionism, Bloomsbury—all point to aspects of modernism, even if the aims or assumptions of any one "ism" or group were often in direct opposition to those of another.

The two major directions in modernism in prewar Britain can be associated either with *Blast*, the journal founded in 1914 by Pound and Wyndham Lewis, or with Bloomsbury, the area in London where a group of friends, of similar beliefs, sensibilities, and Cambridge connections wrote and painted—Woolf, Strachey, Vanessa Bell, and Roger Fry, among others. Forster was also a part of Bloomsbury, but as with all his affiliations, he was something of an outsider even when he was inside. Both groups believed in the integration of the arts, but there is a considerable difference between the manifesto-issuing, heroic, protofascist, "high" modernism of the *Blast* group, with its vision of the individual as a "durable, imposing . . . harder machine,"[12] and the domestic, "low" modernism of Bloomsbury. The latter linked ethics and aesthetics in terms directly opposed to the heroic modernists. Bloomsbury, following G. E. Moore's formulation in *Principia Ethica* (1903), believed that "personal affection and the appreciation of what is beautiful in Art or Nature are good in themselves."[13] Bloomsbury worked in the impressionist and psychological modes in contrast to the expressionist and mythological modes of the high modernists.

Whatever their differences, however, all these writers and artists—and others like Joyce and Eliot who cannot be classified clearly, although both were closer to *Blast* than to Bloomsbury—felt themselves in the midst of a process of social and cultural change that was already well under way by the start of the First World War, called "the Great War" in Britain. The war thus accelerated and threw into relief what had begun some 5 to 10 years earlier. But its extraordinary violence and waste, its grotesque theater of the absurd where hundreds of thousands of men died in the Belgian mud, victims of the madness and incompetence of their generals, made it almost impossible to retain any prewar innocence after 11 November 1918. The prevailing mood of the writing of the postwar

8

years is one of cynicism and alienation. Pound's *Hugh Selwyn Mauberley* provides an apt figure for the new writing:

> The age demanded an image
> Of its accelerated grimace,
> Something for the modern stage,
> Not, at any rate, an Attic grace.[14]

Eliot's *The Waste Land*, a poem he claimed would have been the same had there been no war, is nonetheless suffused with the images, though displaced by myth and indirection, of that war. As old beliefs had crumbled, so had old forms. Genre boundaries were blurred; poems and novels were less stable, less authoritative, characterized by the fragmentary and the unfinished. As recent critics have argued, the detached, the provisional, and the hypothetical are the typical modernist stances.[15]

Those qualities describe Forster, too, but not entirely. Thus, *A Passage to India*, when it finally appeared in 1924, may at first glance have seemed rather old-fashioned compared to the new fiction of Joyce and Woolf, for Forster's writing carries the history of the English novel—tea parties, picnics, will the engaged couple marry?—close to its surface. Yet it brings together parts of that tradition that rarely have been linked. Not too many fictions evoke comparisons with both *Moby-Dick* and the novels of Jane Austen. But it is the novel's mingling of those vastly different modes and voices, and in its bleak, unnerving vision, that its peculiar modernity—and its essential antimodernism—can be found.

2

The British Raj and the Writing of *A Passage to India*

Forster published *A Passage to India* in 1924, dedicating it to "Syed Ross Masood and to the seventeen years of our friendship." Without that friendship, as Forster often remarked, there would have been neither passage nor *A Passage to India.* "My own debt to him is incalculable. He woke me up out of my suburban and academic life, showed me new horizons and a new civilization, and helped me towards the understanding of a continent. . . . He made everything real and exciting as soon as he began to talk, and seventeen years later when I wrote *A Passage to India* I dedicated it to him out of gratitude as well as out of love, for it would never have been written without him."[1]

The India that Masood introduced Forster to was the India of the Muslim Revival that had begun in the 1860s with the founding of the Scientific Society by Masood's grandfather, Sir Syed Ahmed Khan, a major figure in the late nineteenth-century Islamic reform movement. The main goal of the society was to translate Western scientific research into Urdu. His grandfather's greatest achievements were the establishment of the Muhammadan Anglo-Oriental College at Aligarh in 1875 and the Muhammadan Anglo-Oriental Educational Conference in 1886. Politically he was an active supporter of the British and an opponent of the emergent Hindu National Congress. Masood's father was a Cambridge-educated jurist, and Masood himself read law at Oxford and practiced it for some years after his return to India, before he became director of public education in Hyderabad. Thus, both a strong connection to Britain and a commitment to the reform of religion, education, and politics are the defining characteristics of the Muslim Indian world that Forster entered on his first voyage.

In his visits to two of the Native States in 1912 and 1921 Forster also got a glimpse of aristocratic Hindu India. He also spent time with his fellow British in their clubs, offices, and homes. The novel reflects this personal experience as well as his considerable research into Indian history and culture and into the history of the British in India. Much of this contextual material is assumed in the novel. References to the Indian Mutiny, for example, are not explicated, while the reasons for and the form of the British presence are not given. How did the British arrive at their "sensibly planned" civil station overlooking Chandrapore, and how did they gain the power to call Dr. Aziz from his dinner table and to humiliate him when he answers their call? A brief historical account of the British in India should help to answer these questions and to provide a context for understanding those events of the second decade of the twentieth century that the novel recapitulates, revises, and inserts itself into.

THE BRITISH IN INDIA

For well over 200 years, beginning with a charter granted to it in 1600 by Queen Elizabeth, the East India Company represented British interests in India. A trading company with centers across India, it gradually took on many of the functions of government—building forts, maintaining armies, and overseeing conquered territories. In 1858 the company was abolished and the Crown took control of the colony. The preexisting administrative structure remained operative, with some changes in detail provided in a succession of India Acts, until the Government of India Act of 1935 established a framework for the participation of both the central government and the provincial governments in the administration of the country. This process was not completed until 1947 with the final granting of independence to India as a predominantly Hindu state and the simultaneous creation of a Muslim Pakistan.

From the early nineteenth century on, the administration of British holdings and interests was in the charge of the Indian Civil Service. It consisted of about 1,000 "civilians," university graduates (primarily from Oxford and Cambridge) who, after 1853, were chosen on the basis of competitive examinations. In theory, Indians were allowed to compete for places in the Indian Civil Service, but since the examinations were held in London, only a minuscule number were able to do so. The civil servants' functions were administrative and judicial, and they were directly responsible to the Collector (Deputy Commissioner) who was in charge of the district (a subdivision of a province). The Indian Civil Service and the military were the most important of the services, but there were various others including police, medicine, and education. Through the early part of the century "Anglo-Indian" was the term used to describe the British in India—civil servants, the military, merchants, and missionaries—and "Eurasian" was used for those born in India of mixed European and Asian parentage. In 1911, however, "Anglo-Indian" was designated as the replacement for "Eurasian." Nonetheless, the old usage remained dominant among the British at least until World War II, when "Indo-British" began to replace it. In this study I follow Forster's practice and use "Anglo-Indian" in its earlier sense.[2]

The country the British ruled consisted of vast territories acquired by conquest during the seventeenth and eighteenth centuries. By 1805, Britain had control of the northern provinces, Bengal, and all of eastern and most of southern India. By the third quarter of the nineteenth century, it had extended its territories by conquest, annexation, and absorption to include Sind, the Punjab, Burma, Assan, and Oudh. As well, it had a looser but still controlling role to play in the nominally independent Native States (also called the Princely States) of the Rajputana, Central India, Hyderabad, Mysore, and Madras.

To reach this position the British had had to eliminate their commercial rivals among other colonizing European countries (especially Portugal, France, and the Netherlands), as well as the forces of the Mogul Empire and of the Maratha Confederacy. Babur's invasion of India two centuries earlier in 1523 had led to the founding of the Mogul Empire. That conquest was consolidated by his grandson Akbar, who adroitly managed a complex empire that brought Hindu Rajputs into high office in a Muslim kingdom (the two emperors, but particularly Babur, are the subject of Aziz's proud reveries in Forster's novel). Many of the formal structures of that empire—its administrative bureaucracy, which included a significant number of foreigners, and its systems of land measurement, crop estimation, and revenue collection—were taken over by the British when their empire replaced that of the Moguls. The historian Percival Spear has studied the close affinity between the early British merchant official and his Mogul predecessor, observing that "the arrogance of the Mughal *nawab* was proverbial, so that no surprise was caused by comparable conduct on the part of their British successors. But the Mughals treated each other the same way they treated the Hindus. What eventually caused complaint against the British was the discovery that they had one code of behavior amongst themselves and another for their relations with Indians."[3] It is in that disparity that Forster situates the social and political analysis of his novel.

Most of the Mogul empire's 150 years were peaceful and, artistically, extraordinarily productive. However, its continual expansion, especially southward during the seventeenth century, led to a series of wars with the Hindu Maratha Confederacy that continued through the eighteenth century. At the same time the British were increasing their territorial base, their most important victory being the defeat of the nawab of Bengal at Plassey in 1757. Although the Maratha Confederacy was not entirely subdued until 1805, the East India Company had by then consolidated both economic and political power. Its holdings were immensely profitable, especially the indigo plantations, and its profits soared after 1765 when it acquired the power to collect taxes in Bengal. In England this was the period of the *nabob,* a contemptuous term derived from the Mogul title *nawab,* which was applied to Englishmen who made fortunes in India and returned to purchase large estates (and parliamentary seats).[4] However, not all in England viewed this unprecedented profit making and taking with pleasure. The historian Fernand Braudel quotes Sir George Saville in 1777 speaking out against the East India Company and "the public thefts to which he did not wish in any way to be a party."[5]

Beginning in 1773, the Regulating Acts were passed by the British Parliament to define the political and commercial functions of the company. The 1773 Act established the position of Governor-General, who as viceroy was the chief representative of the Crown in India. The most significant of these acts was the India Act of 1784 that established the Board of Control in London (later the Council of India, the post of president of the board becoming secretary of state for India) to supervise the company's affairs. Although the primary relationship between Britain and India during the first half of the nineteenth century was economic and paternalistic, there was a strong reformist component to several of the administrations, especially Lord William Bentinck's governor-generalship (1828–35). Bentinck allowed Indians to enter the judicial service, allowed the use of the vernacular in pleadings before the court, and introduced legislation to prohibit suttee (the ritual self-immolation of widows on their husbands' funeral pyres). It was also during this period that Thomas Babington Macaulay, the British historian and literary critic who had been appointed to the Supreme Council of India in 1834, worked to free the press from licensing restrictions. He was also instrumental in passing legislation that was vehemently resisted by the British (they called it the "Black Act") to deny them special courts in India.

Yet all Macaulay's and Bentinck's actions were based on British interests and beliefs. Macaulay's intervention in the debate over the language of instruction, for example, between those who argued for the use of Indian languages and those who supported English (the latter including prominent Indian intellectuals such as Ram Mohan Roy), was the deciding factor in the decision to make English the official language of instruction in India. "I have no knowledge of either Sanskrit or Arabic," he wrote, "but I am quite ready to take the Oriental learning at the valuation of the Orientalists [that is, European scholars] themselves. I have never found one among them who could deny that a single shelf of a good European library was worth the whole native literature of India and Arabia."[6] Forster's remark in a 1953 review concerning a similar observation that Macaulay had made about Hindu art ("hideous and ignoble") in contrast to Greek art ("beautiful and majestic"), identifies a crucial assumption underlying British rule: "He never thought of learning from India, he only thought of improving her, and since Indian art did not strike him as improving, it had to be destroyed."[7]

The underlying belief that guided Macaulay—and, indeed, nearly all British administrators, no matter how enlightened—can be found in his assertion that "we know that India cannot have a free government. But she may have the next best thing—a firm and impartial despotism."[8] The belief that despotism could be impartial and self-evidently beneficial to the governed derives directly from the ideological underpinnings of British imperial practice. Raghavan Iyer has identified these as the Burkean doctrine of imperial trusteeship, the utilitarian doctrine derived from Bentham and the Mills of state activity, the Platonic idea of rulers as wise guardians, and the evangelical belief in the benefit of spreading the gospel to the heathen. The result, according to Iyer, was "a centralized, enlightened despotism that was transformed in time into an elaborate, autocratic bureaucracy."[9]

The event that more than any other marks the shift from "enlightened despotism" to "autocratic bureaucracy" was the Indian Mutiny that began at the garrison at Meerut near Delhi in May 1857 and continued throughout the northern and central parts of India for the next 14 months. Its immediate cause was the belief on the part of the native soldiers (sepoys) that the cartridges they were using were greased with beef or pork fat. Although this may not have been true—and, in any event, when the soldiers complained they were given ungreased cartridges that they could prepare themselves—it provided a ready symbol of the fact that the British could wantonly disrupt their customs and beliefs. In fact one could argue that the mutiny was partly a consequence of the purportedly benevolent motives behind the earlier reform policies. Benjamin Disraeli did precisely that when he spoke in Parliament two months after the outbreak of the mutiny: "I would range under three heads the various causes which have led . . . to a general discontent among all classes . . . first, our forcible destruction of native authority; next, our disturbance of the settlement of property; and thirdly, our tampering with the religion of the people."[10]

If bullets symbolized British attitudes toward Indian customs, the massacre of the British at Cawnpore (Kanpur) by the sepoys under their leader Nana Sahib at the end of June became the representative event in all British accounts of the mutiny and the justification for the most violent acts in its suppression. That the massacre might have been in retaliation for British actions in early

June at Benares and Allahabad, as some historians have argued, was not even considered in contemporary British accounts, which pictured the natives as vicious and treacherous, deserving of the most repressive treatment. Nonetheless, while holding on to this generalizing stereotype, especially for the Bengali, the British attempted to placate some of their other Indian subjects, particularly the princes of the Native States and the large landholders. To that end, the governor-general, Lord Lytton, whose proposal for an Indian peerage had not succeeded, set up a Statutory Service for Indians in 1879, but on the basis of social position, not competition. The British understood the utility of maintaining the political allegiance of the princes who had for the most part remained loyal to Britain during the mutiny. The comment in 1876 of the British Foreign Secretary Robert Salisbury to Disraeli, then prime minister, sums up British attitudes precisely: "Whether the aristocracy themselves are very powerful may be doubted, and any popularity we may achieve with them is not much to lean upon in a moment of trial. But it is good as far as it goes; their good will and co-operation, if we can obtain it, will at all events serve to hide to the eyes of our own people and perhaps, of the growing literary class in India the nakedness of the sword on which we rely."[11] Simultaneously, however, there was a general hardening of Anglo-Indian attitudes, as illustrated by the failure in 1883 of an act that would have allowed Indian judges to try European offenders in rural areas.

In such a brief summary it is impossible to convey the distinctive features of the various administrations from the 1880s through the first two decades of the twentieth century. Some were more authoritarian than others, and some were more concerned with material progress, with the building of roads and railroads, of hospitals and schools. However, independent of the viceroy's identity and place of residence (Calcutta until 1911, then Delhi), the business of rule was carried out by the Indian Civil Service, a large and bureaucratic structure preoccupied with administrative tasks "almost to the exclusion of broader political concerns such as the introduction of some measure of self government" (Wurgaft, 23). Nevertheless, during this period the first stirrings of large-scale political organization and resistance occurred.

In 1885 the Indian National Congress held its first meeting. Composed of writers, journalists, lawyers, and businessmen, it was at the start more a discussion group than a political party and had the apparent support of the viceroy, Lord Dufferin. However, such patronage did not last long as the Congress became more vocal in its criticism and demands; by 1904 the demand for eventual self-government had become official policy of the Congress. Divisions within the party between moderates such as Gokhale who were willing to work within the structure of British rule and militants such as Tilak, Ghose, and Pal, who urged immediate confrontation with the British, first became apparent over the British decision to partition the province of Bengal in 1905. Although that decision was rescinded in 1911 the intervening years saw considerable political unrest including attacks led by Tilak and Pal in Bengal and in western India.

The Muslim position was quite different. The Muslim League from its founding in 1906 had urged loyalty to the British government while arguing for the protection and entrenchment of Muslim rights against the Hindus, a position that "received encouragement from the British government as it presented them with a very handy and effective weapon to weaken nationalist forces."[12] The Muslim League, for example, supported the partition of Bengal, an arrangement that was economically advantageous to the Muslims of East Bengal. According to some historians, it was the British rescinding of partition under strong Hindu pressure that made the Muslim League realize that it could not count on British support and hence made it more willing to join with the Congress.[13]

In response to the growing political unrest and pressure for self-government (swaraj), the British brought in several halfway measures, such as the Minto-Morley Indian Councils Act of 1909, which opened membership of provincial councils to Indians, and the 1917 Montagu-Chelmsford reforms. These reforms, sponsored by Edwin Montagu, then secretary of state in India, and Lord Chelmsford, viceroy, were incorporated in the 1919 Government of India Act but were not implemented until 1921. The act called for dyarchy, a parallel structure that reserved for Indians certain less important functions of government. The structure never worked, proving to be, in Montagu's own words, "much too small for the situation in India."[14] Similar proposals were equally useless—for example, the Chamber of Princes, which Forster referred to in a 1922 essay as "one of the many still born children of Lord Chelmsford" (*AH*, 336). Still, some of Montagu's reforms had far-reaching effects, in particular the admission of large numbers of Indians into the civil service.

1919 was a critical year in the evolution of modern India, and it provides the most immediate historical context for Forster's novel. It was the year of the bill proclaiming dyarchy, of the deadly influenza epidemic that had raged worldwide for several years, of the Rowlatt Acts and the subsequent unrest leading to Gandhi's first major campaign of civil disobedience (*satyagraha*), and of the Amritsar Massacre. The Rowlatt Acts, which were never implemented, would have allowed judges to try political cases without juries, to admit in evidence statements made by the dead or the absent, which thus could not be subject to cross-examination, and to allow internment without trial. Gandhi, who had returned from South Africa in 1915 where he had led civil disobedience campaigns in support of the rights of Indians in that country, led the resistance to the Rowlatt Acts in 1919, primarily by means of the *hartal*, a series of one-day work stoppages and fasts.

Protest spread very rapidly and there were acts of violence on both sides. In Amritsar on 10 April a crowd rioted when they were not allowed to enter the European cantonment and an English woman, Marcella Sherwood, was badly beaten. (It is interesting to observe, in light of Forster's novel, that after the attack she refused government compensation and wrote to the *Times* to point out that she had been saved by the parents of her Indian students.[15]) Although public assemblies were prohibited following the riot, a large crowd gathered at the Jallianwalla Bagh in Amritsar on 13 April. It was an enclosed space and the crowd had no means of escape when British troops under General Dyer opened fire, killing nearly 400 and wounding over 1,000. This was followed by a period of martial law that lasted nearly two months. One of the punishments, Dyer's infamous "crawling order" that all Indians entering the road where Marcella Sherwood had been attacked were to crawl on all fours, has a direct echo in Forster's text.

Officially, Dyer's actions were condemned and he was relieved of his post. But for the civil servants and the military, as well as for a large portion of the British press, he was a hero for whom they raised £26,000 as a testimonial. For them the Amritsar Massacre revived all the fears and instinctive responses of the Indian Mutiny over 60 years earlier. For Gandhi and the Indian National Congress, however, the event marked the end of any policy of conciliation or compromise, and 1920 saw the beginning of the Non-Cooperation movement, a joining of the Congress with the Muslim League in a Hindu-Muslim entente. The immediate issue was support of the Khilifat movement, begun in India in 1920 by Muhammed and Shaukat Ali to resist the partitioning of Turkey after the First World War, as outlined by the Treaty of Sèvres, and to restore the Turkish sultan, who was considered the head of Islam, to his former position. For, in Gandhi's words, "no influence, direct or indirect, over the Holy Places of Islam will ever be tolerated by Indian Mussalmans" (Das 1977, 133). Both for political expedience and because a vision of Hindu-Muslim unity was central to Gandhi's beliefs, the two groups joined together in anti-British agitation.

It was a fragile entente. There was too long a past history of divided communities. Thus the Non-Cooperation movement did not continue long past the communal riots between Muslims and Hindus that flared up in 1922, especially in southern India, and Gandhi's imprisonment the same year. Forster's second visit to India took place in 1921, just at that moment of uneasy balance between the two communities, when anti-British activity was increasing. His primary vantage point, however, was in a princely state, so that he was a spectator to, but largely protected from, the unrest in the country.

FORSTER IN INDIA AND IN EGYPT
AND THE WRITING OF THE NOVEL

Forster's interest in India began in 1906 with his friendship with Masood. Engaged as his Latin tutor, he was to help prepare him for entrance to Oxford. Forster, 10 years his senior, had read classics at Cambridge and had recently completed the introduction and notes to a new translation of the *Aeneid*. His literary career was on the verge of attracting attention. *Where Angels Fear to Tread* had already been published and both *The Longest Journey* and *A Room with a View* were well under way. A few years later, in 1910, with the publication of his fourth novel, *Howards End*, Forster was considered among the most important of the new novelists, and he was earning money besides. As he wrote to Masood in November 1910, "My book is selling so well that I shall probably make enough money by it to come to India" (Lago and Furbank, 1:118).

By that time, the relationship between them had grown very close; indeed, Forster had fallen in love with Masood. Although his love was not reciprocated (Masood seems to have been entirely heterosexual), the friendship remained deep and affectionate. Consequently, even before his first visit, there was an emotional charge to Forster's connection to India, a charge that was to remain in the writing where Masood reemerges (at least his essential nature, not the details of his daily life) in the very different body and in the rather different social position of Dr. Aziz.

Forster had begun thinking about visiting India in early 1910, and Masood certainly encouraged him. Shortly after receiving Forster's letter about the success of *Howards End*, Masood wrote: "You know my great wish is to get *you* to write a book on India, for I feel convinced from what I know of you that it will be a great book. I do not wish to flatter you in any way but the fact is that you are about the only Englishman in whom I have come across true sentiment & that, too, real sentiment even from the Oriental point of view. . . . I say Go on Go on improving your imagination & with it your power of physically feeling the difficulties of another. This is what we call *Tarass*" (Furbank, 194).

There was another personal connection important both for itself and as it opened an aspect of Hindu India for Forster. That was his friendship with Malcolm Darling, a member of the Indian Civil Service from 1904, and a friend of Forster from their undergraduate days at Cambridge. It was through Darling that Forster met the Rajah of Dewas Senior for a brief visit in 1912 and to whose court he returned some nine years later for a six-month stay as private secretary. In the 1942 Everyman edition of *A Passage to India*, Forster altered the dedication to include, after Masood's name, that of the Rajah as well: "I desire in this edition to join with his name that of His Highness Sir Tukoji Rao Puar III, K. C. S. I., Maharajah of Dewas State Senior, whom I knew as Bapu Sahib. Both these friends are now dead. Masood lies near his grandfather, the founder of the University of Aligarh. The ashes of Bapu Sahib are scattered in southern India, far from his kingdom and beloved home."[16] Remarkably, both men died in the same year, 1937.

The Rajah of Dewas Senior (the title of Maharajah was granted later) is the principal subject of another book Forster wrote many years later about India, *The Hill of Devi* (1953). An invaluable sourcebook for a reading of *A Passage to India*, it is also—in the words of Santha Rama Rau, the novelist and playwright who adapted *A Passage to India* for the stage in 1960—"a tribute to ghosts."[17] In it Forster gathers, edits, and stitches together letters he wrote home to family and friends during both his trips. It is focused primarily on the Rajah so that it is, of all the genres it participates in, most nearly a biography of a man Forster described as someone he was "tempted to call . . . a saint, but saints are supposed to be reliable, anyhow by the British, and the Maharajah certainly wasn't that" (*Hill,* 297). From the letters themselves as well as from their tidied-up and excerpted versions in *The Hill of Devi* and from the journals Forster kept on his trips, one can get a fairly comprehensive picture of the raw materials and the process of their shaping and transformation that yielded—finally and with much effort and frustration—the text we are now examining.

On his first trip, Forster was for the most part a tourist. He traveled with several English friends and did the sights: Bombay, Aligarh, Lahore, Peshwar, Simla, Agra, Gwalior, Chhatarpur, Bhopal, Ujain, Indore, Dewas, Allahabad, Benares, Patna, the Barabar Caves, Buddh Gaya, Lucknow, Amritsar, Patiala, Delhi, Jaipur, Jodhpur, Hyderabad, Aurangbad, back to Bombay, a boat to Karachi, and another boat to Marseilles for a month's travel in France before returning home. He saw the Taj Mahal, rode an elephant, visited famous caves and temples. He met a variety of Anglo-Indians, some relatively sympathetic like the novelists Sara Jeanette Duncan whom he visited in Simla or Edmund Candler in Patiala; others far less so, like his dinner companion on 4 January 1913 at Allahabad, who said, "I despise the native at the bottom of my heart" (*Hill,* 172).

He spent time with Masood at Patna, which, along with the adjacent British civil station quarter of Bankipore, suggested many of the details of the Chandrapore of the novel. And through Masood, he met in Delhi several of the leading intellectuals and activists of the Muslim Revival—Mohammed and Shaukat Ali and

M. A. Ansari, for example. He visited an Indian friend from Cambridge, Abu Saeed Mizra, a magistrate in Hyderabad, who brought him to a court room where he saw a "Punkah boy, seated at end of table; [who] had the impassivity of Atropos," an image that reappears intact in the novel, as does their ride together, where, anticipating the last scene of Forster's text, "S. burst out against the English. 'It may be fifty or five hundred years but we shall turn you out' " (*Hill,* 223).

And, of course, the Barabar Caves. Oddly, while he describes going to see them and is full of circumstantial detail in his long journal-letter to his mother, he does not seem to have experienced anything extraordinary there—quite the contrary: "The caves are cut out of solid granite: A small square doorway and an oval hall inside. This sounds dull, but the granite has been so splendidly polished that they rank very high among caves for cheerfulness" (*Hill,* 188). But the elaborately decorated Buddhist Caves at Ellora, which he visited near the end of his stay, impressed him quite differently: "Supporting cornice of blackened monsters—elephants, griffons, tigers who rend. The great mild face of a goddess, doing cruelty, fades into the pit-wall." But a few days later he adds, "Their impression is already fading, I think because there is no beauty and I do not believe in the devil, whose palace they are. They are Satanic masterpieces to terrify others" (*Hill,* 225, 227).

That journal entry is typical of the way Forster recorded his experiences—a response balanced between his own sensibility and his attempt to see the world though others' eyes, to follow, as he described it in *The Hill of Devi,* "the prompting of the eye and the imagination" (*Hill,* 42). Indeed, one member of the Dewas court remarked, "We are greatly pleased by your so good nature. We have not met an Englishman like you previously" (*Hill,* 67). These comments were made in 1921; in 1912 he had remained more on the outside of the world of the native state, which struck him, at least in Dewas, as rather like a "Gilbert and Sullivan opera" (*Hill,* 6). However, his visit a few weeks before to the Native State of Chhatarpur seemed to have made a deeper impression on him. Both Chhatarpur itself, insofar as it was to yield the physical aspects of Mau, the setting of the novel's third section, and its Maharajah, insofar as he would provide much of the material for Godbole, formed an important part of the experience of that first trip.

As Robin Lewis suggests, "Forster has taken the Maharajah as his principal model, divesting him of his Western traits and retaining only the core of the ruler's character—his search for union with the divine as a means of attaining universal love,"[18] which is the underlying principle of the Brahman practice that Godbole exemplifies. The name, however, comes from an entirely different source. For Forster has left a record of an evening party in 1913 where he had "talked about Indian music to a Mr. Godbole—what a name!—and afterwards we took a walk through the Public Gardens where he sang songs to me. There are scales appropriate for all hours of the day. That for the evening was the Scale of C major, but with F sharp in it instead of F" (*Hill*, 203). The Godbole of the novel remarks that his song "is composed in a raga appropriate to the present hour, which is the evening."[19] In the text, however, this statement is made at the collision point of every system, sensibility, and point of view. There is no agreeable stroll in a public garden, but rather the imploring of a deity who "neglects to come" and the uneasy, unsatisfied dispersal of all the guests.

On his return to England Forster tried to turn the past year into a book, a process he described in a talk he gave in 1959: "I began the book after my 1912 visit, wrote half a dozen chapters of it and stuck. I was clear about the chief characters and the racial tension, had visualized the scenery and had foreseen that something crucial would happen in the Marabar Caves. But I hadn't seen far enough" (*Hill*, 298). Moreover, before leaving for India, he had run into difficulty with an entirely different novel, *Arctic Summer*, which he had begun in late 1911. It was, as he wrote from India to a friend, the Irish novelist Forrest Reid, "too like *Howards End* to interest me; a contrast again; between battle and work; the chief figure a Knight errant born too late in time who finds no clear issue to which to devote himself; . . . I want something beyond the field of action and behaviour; the waters of the river that rises from the middle of the earth to join the Ganges and the Jumna where they join. India is full of such wonders, but she can't give them to me" (Lago and Furbank, 1:187–88). Thus, despite the initial burst of creative energy in the fall of 1913, he found himself with two unfinished and blocked books on his hands.

Or really three. For it is just at this time that he began to write *Maurice*, the novel in which he moved away from what he called "the swish of skirts" of *Howards End*—that is, the marriage conventions of the traditional novel—to celebrate homosexual love by an enlarging of those very conventions. *Maurice* was not left unfinished, but finishing it did not release the other two, especially as it could not have been published easily in 1914, so that, finished or not, it remained in his desk drawer with the others.

At the same time the First World War had begun, a conflict about which Forster had no illusions and certainly no reflexive or automatic patriotism: "The newspapers still talk about glory but the average man, thank God, has got rid of that illusion . . . whichever side wins, civilization in Europe will be pipped for the next 30 years. Don't indulge in Romance here, Malcolm, or suppose that an era of jolly little nationalities is dawning. We shall be much too occupied with pestilence and poverty to reconstruct" (letter to Malcolm Darling, Lago and Furbank, 1:214). Forster's response was to leave England for Alexandria to work as a searcher for the Red Cross. His initial plan had been to join an ambulance unit, for, as he wrote to Masood, "All one can do in this world of maniacs is to pick up the poor tortured broken people and try to mend them" (Lago and Furbank, 1:224). His job as a searcher was to talk to the wounded in hospital to find out what he could about those who had been reported as missing. He also read to the soldiers and wrote their letters and on his own time entered as much as possible into the life of the polyglot, cosmopolitan city whose chief figure, in Forster's eyes, was the Greek poet Cavafy.

Cavafy enters directly into Forster's two Alexandria books—*Pharos and Pharillon*, the collection of essays about the city's impressive past and diminished present that he gathered from the articles he had published in the *Egyptian Mail* and in some English journals over the nearly four years he spent there, and *Alexandria: A History and a Guide*. Both books have as a centerpiece, as the text that links the city's past with her present, Cavafy's poem "The God Abandons Antony." What Forster found particularly congenial in Cavafy, who in Forster's phrase stood "motionless at a slight angle to the universe"[20]—a characterization that has often been applied to Forster himself—was his ability to "convey the obscurity, the poignancy, that sometimes arises together out of the past, entwined into a single ghost" (*PP*, 94). His influence on Forster was complex and deep and has been very well charted by Jane Lagoudis

Pinchin in *Alexandria Still:* the similarity of their sensibilities, their ability to inhabit the past, and most important of all their belief in friendship. "For Cavafy . . . and sometimes for Forster, the mystery of the divine, the religion of love, sings forth in the human form— where sense verges into spirit."[21]

Cavafy's openness about his homosexuality was also an important part of Forster's Alexandrian education. And so was the romantic and, for the first time, fully physical relationship that he formed with Mohammed el Adl, which lasted until Mohammed died from tuberculosis in 1922. *Pharos and Pharillon,* published in 1923, carries an allusive dedication to him as "Hermes Psychopompos," conductor of the souls of the dead, "two words in Greek that fit book and him extraordinarily well," as Forster wrote in a letter to his close friend Florence Barger.[22] As a ghostly presence, Mohammed lingers in the uncanny landscape of *A Passage to India.* There he joins the other ghosts, notably Mrs. Moore, but he is also part of the living, as his memory deepens and complicates Forster's portrayal of Aziz, particularly in his friendship with Fielding.

Both during his stay in Alexandria and on his return to England, Forster followed the political situation very closely. In 1920, he publicly entered the debate on the question of self-government for Egypt in a pamphlet that he wrote at the urging of Leonard Woolf for the Labour Research Department of the Fabian Society. It is an interesting document to read alongside *A Passage to India,* for while it is anti-imperial, it does not entirely give up on the idea of empire. Rather, it criticizes the inhuman form Britain's imperial aspirations have taken: "Before the war was over the country side had experienced, under British auspices, many of the exactions of an Oriental despotism; and as prices rose and pneumonic influenza took its toll, the misery and discontent increased. . . . During the winter of 1918–19 the natives, including the peasantry, became definitely anti-British."[23] He agrees with the Fabian Society's recommendations for mandate status for Egypt under the League of Nations but seems dubious about the success of such an arrangement. In a letter to Leonard Woolf, he made his hesitation clearer: "the best severely practical solution that I can see is that Egypt should be nominally and forcibly but not uncomfortably part of the British empire: i.e. what Milner says but doesn't of course mean. The ideal solution is contained in your recommendations, but I feel that they rest upon what is, and will remain, air."[24] In the pamphlet he expresses regret over the lost opportunities of earlier national movements, for "thus perished a moment, which, if treated sympathetically, might have set Egypt upon the path of constitutional liberty" (*Egypt*, 4). Instead, Egypt was ruled by officials like Lord Cromer, who "had a profound distrust of Orientals" (*Egypt*, 4), and Lord Milner, who "believed that the world would be happier if it were ruled by the British upper middle classes" (*Egypt*, 7).

These are precisely the attitudes that underlie Forster's portrayal of the British in India. But for all that he unmasks their hypocrisies and pretensions, the analysis is complicated by a residual reluctance to give up on his side, on Britain, entirely. Indeed, as he wrote in a letter to his mother from India in 1921, after he had left Dewas to spend the remaining time with Masood, India is a place "where we have done much good and have rights, and where our sudden withdrawal would be a disaster" (*Hill*, 343). When he wrote this, he had, of course, just spent six months at Dewas where "there is no anti-British feeling. It is Gandhi whom they dread and hate" (*Hill*, 55). Forster did not share this feeling toward Ghandi, but one could argue that at this point he did not fully grasp the extent and depth of the movement for self-government, or the degree to which such states as Dewas and Chhatarpur had become anachronisms.

Forster went to India in March 1921 because the possibility fortuitously offered itself—the Rajah of Dewas Senior needed a replacement secretary for six months—and it seemed to promise a means of reviving the India novel he had put aside almost a decade earlier. The latter did not quite happen, as Forster recalled in *The Hill of Devi*: "I began this novel before my 1921 visit, and took out the opening chapters with me, with the intention of continuing them. But as soon as they were confronted with the country they purported to describe, they seemed to wilt and go dead and I could do nothing with them. I used to look at them of an evening in my room at Dewas, and felt only distaste and despair. The gap between India remembered and India experienced was too wide" (*Hill*, 99). In the same year that he published *The Hill of Devi* he gave an interview in which he elaborated that point: "I began it [*A Passage to India*] in 1912, and then came the war. I took it with me when I returned to India in 1921, but found what I had written wasn't India at all. It was like sticking a photograph on a picture."[25]

The frustration implicit in these remarks is not readily audible in *The Hill of Devi* itself. For the past had receded by then, so that the 1953 text is largely a cheerful, bemused, and amusing account of the intricacies, confusions, and mysterious doings of the Dewas court. The central figure is the Rajah, set in a landscape and a world long since vanished; it is largely an act of homage. Forster is, of course, an important presence in these pages, especially as he witnesses Gokul Ashtami, the eight-day festival celebrating the birth of Krishna, which he incorporates directly into the final section of the novel. But his interior experiences are left largely unrecorded. Elizabeth Heine points out in her excellent notes and introduction to *The Hill of Devi* that an observation that Forster made in an unpublished memoir, written sometime after the publication of *A Passage to India*, provides an interesting clue both to that interior experience and to Forster's conception of the text. He was glad to be able to go then, he wrote, for "I should get . . . the experience of the Hot Weather for which I was anxious" (*Hill*, 375). Heine relates this to Forster's association of the tripartite division of the novel ("Mosque," "Caves," "Temple") with "the three seasons of the cold weather, the hot weather and the Rains, which divide the Indian year" that he outlined in his notes to the 1942 Everyman edition. And she more particularly connects this linkage of caves and heat to another unpublished text, the "Kanaya" memoir, included in her edition. There Forster records his covert sexual experiences with the Rajah's servants at the Dewas court and his attendant confusion and guilt, made the more complicated and intense by the Rajah's protection of Forster despite his disapproval. In a letter to a reviewer, Forster wrote: "Then there is an unpublished section, which would have made H. H.'s claims to sainthood clearer. That couldn't go in because it couldn't" (*Hill*, ix). Thus, at the center of *The Hill of Devi*, there is an omission, a gap, that precisely parallels the gap—the empty cave, the unanswerable question—at the center of the novel.

Although Forster had not stopped thinking about India and wrote many articles and reviews on Indian subjects after returning to England, it was largely because of Leonard Woolf's insistent encouragement that he finally got back to work on the novel. In a diary entry for 12 April 1922, he wrote, "At Leonard's advice have read my India fragment with a view to continuing it. . . . The philosophic scheme of the fragment still suits me. Must try to recover my dormant sense of space. Earthy self-consciousness" (*Ab. PI*, xv). But the difficulties in writing were numerous—the discrepancy between memory and experience, his frustration, his disappointment at not having been able to move it forward while he had been in India, and the enormous social and political changes that had occurred there since his first visit. Added to this was the news of Mohammed el Adl's death that reached him soon after his return. The book that gradually emerged, while it used much of the material of the first draft—the first four chapters and parts of chapters 7, 8, 12, 13, and 14—was quite different in emphasis and outlook from what he had originally planned. "When I began the book," he wrote in a letter to Masood, "I thought of it as a little bridge of sympathy between East and West, but this conception has had to go, my sense of truth forbids anything so comfortable. I think that most Indians, like most English people, are shits, and I am not interested whether they sympathize with one another or not. Not interested as an artist; of course the journalistic side of me still gets roused over these questions, and I have just poured out that part of my soul in an article on India and the Turks for the *Nation*.[26] How these two sides cooperated to produce *A Passage to India* is a problem that recurs in our discussion of the novel.

3

"Expansion . . . Not Completion"

"Fictions are for finding things out and they change as the needs
of sense making change."
　　—Frank Kermode, *The Sense of an Ending*

A Passage to India has no equal in the entire literature of the Raj.[1]
It is, at once, the last colonial and the first postcolonial text. It
inscribes the civilization and assumptions of the conqueror, but at
the same time it refuses to take shelter in the myths that support
that rule. In its passage to India, the novel blurs and complicates
the line between self and other, ruler and ruled. Its imaginative
vision does not patronize but enters this other world to discover it
on its own terms. The intense feeling for place that pervades all
Forster fiction prevents India from disappearing into metaphor,
from being a screen on which Western characters can project their
metaphysical anguish. Rather, India and Indians are realized for
themselves. An Indian reviewer described his sense of relief and
gratitude on first reading the novel: Forster was "the first to raise
grotesque legendary creatures and terracotta figures to the dignity
of human beings" (Gardner, 290). Santh Rama Rau, who adapted
the novel for the stage, observed that "the most astonishing aspect
of the book for many Indians, was that it had the courage to talk
and think from inside of the Indian mind."[2]

　　This is a quality frequently noted by Indian writers. As novelist
Mulk Raj Anand wrote in a letter-essay to Forster on his ninetieth
birthday, "You are perhaps the only Englishman of this century
who came near enough to understanding Indian people." Empha-

sizing the novel's political realism, Anand continued, "apart from the attempt to realise the patterns of Indian civilisation . . . you wished to say one important thing: that there could be no friendship between Indians and Englishmen until Indians were free" (Natwar-Singh, 43). Like many of his generation of Indian writers who wrote in English, Anand felt indebted to Forster: "I could not have started off writing my first book, Untouchable, if I had not noticed your own sympathy for the outcastes of India" (Natwar-Singh, 45). This theme also appears in expatriate Indian writing. Bharati Mukherjee, whose first novel appeared 37 years after Untouchable, said that until she read Forster's novel as a graduate student in America, she had assumed "as a well brought up postcolonial . . . that India and Indians were not worthy of serious literature, that the India I knew had no legitimacy in fiction. The wonder in reading Forster was that forty years before, he had written about a society I thought I could still recognize."[3]

A Passage to India is many things at once—political and metaphysical, social and visionary, skeptical and prophetic. Virginia Woolf, surveying all the novels save Maurice, thought that "satire and sympathy, fantasy and fact, poetry and a prim moral sense" did not easily combine, but that in A Passage to India Forster came close to fusing them into a "single vision," "animating this dense compact body of observation with a spiritual light" (Woolf, 1:344, 351). Her unwillingness to concede complete success was a function of her lack of sympathy with the supernatural and fantastic. She dismissed the stories in The Celestial Omnibus, calling Forster an "uneasy truant in fairyland" (Woolf, 1:347). But it is precisely the element of the fantastic in the stories that Elizabeth Bowen described as "a blaze of unforeseen possibilities." It is an aspect of Forster's imagination that can be generalized to all his fiction, a "magic [that] was not in the matter, but the manner, the telling[:] the creation of a peculiar, electric climate in which anything might happen. . . . With each page, one was in the presence of a growing, not yet definable danger, the blindness of those endangered being part of the spell" (Bowen, 4). Although Bowen was writing of her response to the short story "The Other Kingdom," the words exactly fit the journey to the Marabar in A Passage to India.

Christopher Isherwood, who like Bowen was very much influenced by Forster, also responded to that electricity. His phrase for it was "tea tabling," a technique of toning down so that there is "actually less emphasis laid on the big scenes than on the unimportant ones: that's what's so utterly terrific. It's the completely new kind of accentuation—like a person talking a different language."[4] It is this "different language" that is the novel's most singular accomplishment. The narrator's supple and resonant prose holds his characters' words in a kind of clarifying solution. Far more is implied than said; the smallest gesture holds worlds.

However, Woolf was right to observe that the opposing attributes that she identified do not quite combine. The debatable point is whether they need to. "Only connect," the epigraph to *Howards End*, functions as an exhortation, but it is only accomplished in that novel on the level of wish fulfillment, and even then it is submitted to a skeptical interrogation. The dual impulse that characterizes the modernist text—its simultaneous attraction toward coherence and the fragmentary, toward the transcendental and the contingent, toward the metaphoric and the metonymic—is present in Forster's novel, too. Furthermore, for Forster the creative process itself was based on a structure of antithesis; he always required some contrasting otherness to release his imagination. In the early novels and short stories, it is the freedom of Italy, Cambridge, the greenwood, the still unspoiled countryside, or the realm of fantasy inhabited by Hermes and Pan that is set against the proprieties of suburban England. In *A Passage to India* it is the vast subcontinent so varied in history and geography, in people and belief, that provides this release. In this last extraordinary encounter of sensibility and subject matter, one can observe all the familiar Forsterian qualities—an exacting intelligence and moral vision that moves with ease between the physical and the metaphysical, between fact and fantasy, and an ironic prose that conveys love rather than disdain—but now enlarged and deepened. The result is one of the masterpieces of English prose.

Mulk Raj Anand in his birthday tribute addressed Forster as "one of the great Englishmen, who brought the liberal ideals of generosity, tolerance, and sensitiveness to our country" (Natwar-Singh, 43). But those are the very ideals under siege both in the text and in the clamoring world outside. In *Maurice*, personal relations and love were imagined as sufficient to overcome the barrier of class, but by the time he came to write *A Passage to India*, he had in large measure abandoned such optimism. An awareness of the fragility of these liberal values permeates the language, creating an elegiac mode, appropriate to an "epitaph to liberal humanism," in Benita Parry's apt phrase.[5] Yet the power and the pathos of the novel derive in large part from Forster's attempt to provide an imaginative space for just such notions—generosity, tolerance, personal relations—in a world where they are so clearly insufficient and where their carriers are so little capable of activating them.

The novel is ultimately both bleak and exhilarating in large part because these underlying beliefs are never jettisoned, even though they are finally unavailing. Forster never wrote another novel; nonetheless his reputation and importance on the literary scene increased from year to year. Essays, broadcasts, biographies appeared, all of them animated by those beliefs and values. W. H. Auden's sonnet to Forster just before the outbreak of the Second World War testifies to this: "You promise still the inner life shall pay."[6] But as a novelist he remained silent, as if he had used up his language. Like Godbole in his song to Krishna, he had called, "Come, come, come, come, come, come" and had discovered that "He neglects to come" (PI, 80).

Two years after A Passage to India, Forster gave a series of lectures on fiction at Cambridge University, which were published in 1927 as Aspects of the Novel. His examples were drawn from nearly 300 years of Western fiction, among them novels of Austen and George Eliot, Proust, Gide, Tolstoy, Dostoyevski, and Melville. Much of what he said there, particularly concerning prophecy and fantasy, is directly applicable to his own novels. But it is in his discussion of musical structure in fiction where one finds the most interesting link to A Passage to India: "Expansion. That is the idea the novelist must cling to. Not completion. Not rounding off but opening out. When the symphony is over we feel that the notes and tunes composing it have been liberated, they have found in the rhythm of the whole their individual freedom."[7] We can see this in this last sentence of the novel. Aziz and Fielding ride single file, separated by the rocks of the soil, by history, by the particulars of their diverging lives. But as the musical analogy suggests, there is a connection beyond this separation, expansion beyond this confinement. For, like the notes in a symphony, the characters have "in the rhythm of the whole their individual freedom."

4

Critical Reception

The more than 40 reviews that *A Passage to India* received in England, India, and the United States when it was published in 1924 were nearly all enthusiastic. Although some found it baffling—describing it as "obscure and elusive"—it sold very well: 17,000 copies in Britain and more than 53,000 in the United States by the end of 1924.[1] For many its immediate appeal was its topicality regarding the problem of the British in India. Thus, at first it was received chiefly as a political novel and both reviews and letters to the editor debated its accuracy and fairness.

All noted its evident political engagement. But even reviewers who objected to what they felt were exaggerations and caricature mentioned its complexity of theme and structure and its metaphysical implications. Those who were themselves writers made those implications their main point of praise, although they did not examine them analytically. "It is a political document of the first importance. . . . [B]ut note that it is full of passages of universal beauty, of universal interest," Rebecca West observed in her review (Gardner, 254). L. P. Hartley, like West a novelist, echoed this position in pointing to its political theme but also to its "intensely personal and . . . intensely cosmic" aspects. Hartley noticed, too, a quality that later critics were to elaborate: "[It] is a disturbing, uncomfortable book. . . . There is no emotional repose or security about it" (Gardner, 227). Indeed, Middleton Murry barely noted the political content, "the brilliant, dramatic and absorbing outward fiction." Like Hartley he heard the unease at the book's core, the annihilating echo, and wondered if Forster like his character Mrs.

Moore had entered "the twilight of the double vision" (Gardner, 237). Three years later, in her summing-up of the piece, Virginia Woolf used the phrase "double vision" as her key to the problem of Forster's fiction. The term has haunted much subsequent criticism of *A Passage to India*, usually implying both a divided mind and divided fictional aims.

For the next 10 years Forster's reputation was somewhat in eclipse, although there were sporadic mentions of the novel in review articles on contemporary fiction. There was a renewal of interest in 1934 when Forster published the biography of his friend Goldsworthy Lowes Dickinson and again in 1936 with the publication of a collection of his essays, *Abinger Harvest*. In 1937 two articles that surveyed all his novels appeared, one in Britain by Derek Traversi and one in the United States by Austin Warren, setting the stage for what has been called the Forster revival.[2] Both of these articles emphasize the pessimism of *A Passage to India*; they also insist on its importance both within Forster's canon and for the history of the novel. The first book-length reading appeared the following year by the novelist Rose Macaulay; it is significant chiefly for the reviews it elicited and the subsequent debate on Forster's stature as a novelist. The reviews were remarkably unanimous in calling for a major critical study.

The American critic Lionel Trilling responded to that call in 1943, the year after the publication of the Everyman edition of the novel in England and in the same year as the reissue of the first four novels in the United States. The "revival" had begun. For Trilling, Forster is an exponent of moral realism, a stance of particular urgency in a world at war, but his reading of *A Passage to India* is the book's weakest section. He found it "the most comfortable and even the most conventional of Forster's novels,"[3] although like most critics of this period he underlined the pessimism of its vision, the "sense of separateness [that] broods over the book . . . [and] the cultural differences that keep Indian and Englishman apart" (Trilling, 152). The introduction to the 1942 Everyman edition, by contrast, provided a much more acute and nuanced reading, making a case for the novel's importance that remains entirely cogent. It was a reprint of an essay by Peter Burra, which had first appeared in 1934 but had not been much noticed. Forster's prefatory note to its second reprinting in the 1957 Everyman praised

Burra for "seeing exactly what I was trying to do" (*Ab. PI,* 313).[4] Burra described the novel as "one of the most aesthetically compact books ever written," and he emphasized the caves as "the mystery which is never solved." He noted "the prophetic tone of voice," "the transcendent beauty of the mosque and temple," and "the political passion that describes the disastrous anomaly of the British in India" (*Ab. PI,* 315–27).

In the United States, a 1943 essay by John Crowe Ransom further helped advance Forster's reputation, but he was still considered a relatively minor figure in William York Tindall's *Forces in Modern British Literature* (1947). In the massive *Literary History of England* published the following year, he rated only a muted paragraph.[5] However, he gradually became the subject of critical and scholarly attention with the appearance of his *Collected Short Stories* in 1947 and 1948, *Two Cheers for Democracy* in 1951, *The Hill of Devi* in 1953, and a biography of his great-aunt, *Marianne Thornton,* in 1956. E. K. Brown's *Rhythm in the Novel* (1950) appeared just as this process was beginning. His study relied heavily on Forster's *Aspects of the Novel* in its methodology, treating *A Passage to India* as a prophetic novel with particular emphasis given to the rhythmic interweaving of its themes. In considering Forster's novels along with those of Tolstoy, James, Proust, and Woolf, Brown made strong claims for Forster's importance as a novelist.

Aspects of the Novel—particularly the chapters on people, prophecy, and rhythm—was also central to James McConkey's approach in *The Novels of E. M. Forster* (1957). It was a major study that inaugurated modern Forster scholarship. It is important not only for its subtle analysis of narrative technique but also for setting the terms for subsequent discussions of the significance of Hinduism and of the function of Godbole in the resolution of the novel. For McConkey, "Godbole, more than any other character in the novels, is . . . the Forsterian voice itself" (160). Even before McConkey's book these issues had begun to be debated both in political and philosophical terms. In a much-cited 1954 essay, the Indian writer Nirad Chaudhuri attacked Forster for having a Muslim as his central character and for making Godbole a clown.[6] Although his arguments have been refuted frequently, he represents a recurring position in Forster criticism. Andrew Shonfield repeated it in an influential article in 1968, and in David Shusterman's *The Quest for Certitude* (1965), Godbole is presented as a treacherous character.[7] The relative status of Hindu and Muslim and the nature of the text's representation of its Indian characters are issues that are far from settled. There is considerable difference of opinion among both Indian and Western academic critics.

The relation of Forster's liberal humanism to his view of Hinduism is also a vexed issue. It is related directly to the two questions that defined the dominant critical discourse of the 1960s and 1970s: does the novel endorse unity despite contingency or does it despairingly reveal contingency and chaos despite intimations of potential harmony? Two books that appeared in 1962 line up in suggestive ways on opposite sides of these questions. Frederick Crews's *The Perils of Humanism* takes Trilling's argument concerning the limits of Forster's liberal imagination to its farthest point where neither humanism nor Hinduism avails: "What finally confronts us is an irreparable breach between man's powers and his needs. . . . [B]etween pathetic futility and absolute mystery no middle ground remains for significant action" (163). In contrast, K. W. Grandsen's *E. M. Forster* emphasizes the inclusiveness of Hinduism, and while he notes the darkness in the novel, he sees it move toward unity and reconciliation. A few years later, in George Thomson's *The Fiction of E. M. Forster*, a book notable for its insistence that Forster wrote romances rather than novels, the unity argument is emphatically made: "Through its concrete, sensuous, and visionary unity, Forster's mythic India gives immediate and incarnate assurance that the universe is one" (250).

In its analysis of the tripartite structure of the novel as stages in a spiritual journey, Thomson's 1967 study can be aligned with Wilfred Stone's *The Cave and the Mountain* published in the preceding year. Stone developed an argument that was first broached by Louise Dauner, who treated the cave as archetype—that is, as a part of the collective unconscious.[8] Stone's Jungian analysis takes as its controversial premise that the novels are "dramatic installments in the story of [Forster's] struggle for selfhood." His is the most thorough account of the novel in mythic and symbolic terms, and his conclusions endorse both the unity position ("for all our differences, we are in fact one") and the Hindu solution ("[Hinduism] is the least resistant to the unconscious and the instinctual")[9].

Other important academic books of the decade include John Beer's *The Achievement of E. M. Forster* (1962), Alan Wilde's *Art and Order* (1964), and Frederic McDowell's *E. M. Forster* (1969). McDowell discussed the ironic comedy in the novel, but also followed Stone and Thomson in paying close attention to image and symbol and to the possibility of a Hindu synthesis. Beer placed Forster in a romantic and symbolist tradition and emphasized the importance of Mrs. Moore in his reading of the novel. Wilde's study examined the relation between the aesthetic and the spontaneous in Forster's writing. He saw the novel as moving toward but then away from advocating Hinduism as a solution. In a later essay Wilde took this position much further and argued that *A Passage to India* is a modernist text insofar as "equal and opposed possibilities [are] held in total poise" when the writer withdraws "from chaotic experience . . . into the containment of his art" (Wilde 1979, 38).

In the introduction to his 1985 collection of critical essays on Forster, Wilde described the novel as "the site of conflicting urgencies," a phrase that nicely catches the intensity of the critical debate and suggests as well the greatly varying assumptions and experiences of the critics who have joined that debate. Its terms have not remained constant, either. Having first shifted from the political to the metaphysical, they have now shifted back again, the essentially formalist preoccupations of the studies of the 1960s giving way in the next two decades to more directly social and political concerns. The crucial text here is Benita Parry's *Delusions and Discoveries: Studies on India in the British Imagination 1880–1930* (1972). Her work provides essential contextual material for understanding the British presence in India and the fiction that derived from that encounter. Her reading is also original in its illuminating use of her knowledge of the Jain religion for a discussion of the caves. In a subsequent series of essays she has worked more directly within a postcolonial critique. However, insofar as she reads the text through "its initiation of an oppositional discourse," she resists the postcolonialist move, made by critics like Abdul JanMohamed, of reinserting the novel "into the hegemonic tradition of British Indian literature" (Beer 1985, 28). The ambiguities and contradictions in Forster's vision notwithstanding, Parry finds in the novel "a rare instance of a libertarian perspective on another and subordinated culture produced from within an imperialist metropolis" (Beer 1985, 43).

Our understanding of Forster's experience of India has also been helped greatly by the publication of G. K. Das's *Forster's India* (1977), Oliver Stallybrass's scholarly editions of *A Passage to India* (1978) and *The Manuscripts of "A Passage to India"* (1978); Robin Lewis's *E. M. Forster's Passages to India* (1979); P. N. Furbank's two-volume biography, *E M Forster: A Life* (1977, 1978); Mary Lago and P. N. Furbank's *Selected Letters* (1983, 1985); Elizabeth Heine's edition of *The Hill of Devi* (1983), a volume that also contains other essays on Indian topics, unpublished journals, travel notes, and memoirs; and J. H. Stape's *An E. M. Forster Chronology* (1992).

Forster, of course, also came under renewed scrutiny and reassessment when, following his death in 1970, both *Maurice* and *"The Life to Come" and Other Stories* were published. John Colmer's *The Personal Voice* (1975) was the first major study to integrate this material and Claude Summers's *E. M. Forster* (1983) made it central to his reading of all Forster's fiction. His chapter on *A Passage to India* is a formal and thematic analysis built around the figure of "the friend who never comes." It is grounded on the assumption that, in its explorations of the limitations of human consciousness, the novel "questions the possibility of the very quest for truth that it attempts" (191). Barbara Rosecrance's *Forster's Narrative Vision* (1982) is more narrowly focused on issues of voice and point of view, but it too works within the formalist, New Critical, and liberal humanist assumptions that have dominated the critical discourse since McConkey's 1958 study. Rosecrance develops her argument around a controlling narrative voice that she claims is more pervasive in *A Passage to India* than in his earlier novels, despite its greater distance there from what it is describing. In this omniscient narrator's movement to absolute "detachment from character and reader alike" (236), she finds a movement toward unity, but "a unity whose condition is the withdrawal from human concerns" (232).

A book that takes direct issue with Rosecrance is Bette London's *The Appropriated Voice: Narrative Authority in Conrad, Forster, and Woolf* (1990). London grounds her argument on one of the basic assumptions of postcolonial criticism, that the response from which Forster would dissociate himself is inscribed in his language

(97). Rather than use an omniscient narrator with a distinctive voice, Forster created a voice that, in London's reading, "takes its timbre from whatever voice it is near" (86). His pose of aesthetic supremacy, she argues, "dooms Forster to a position outside" (104). In a detailed reading of the trial scene, she argues that "the political situation is presented as a theatre of self improvisation" (71), an approach that fits into other studies of colonial rule and improvisation, in particular Lewis Wurgaft's *The Imperial Imagination: Magic and Myth in Kipling's India* (1983).

Most of the postcolonial readings assume the text's collusion, even if unwitting, with imperialism. This argument has also been cast in feminist terms: a pervasive antifemale sentiment is identified in the novel's excess of grotesque female characters, and the linkage of racism and rape in the central episode is offered as further evidence of Forster's putative misogyny. Nevertheless, several recent articles that combine feminist and postcolonial approaches assume the validity of the anti-imperialist argument and attempt to reinterpret the text's disruptiveness *for* feminism, even if evidence of misogyny remains. Brenda Silver, for example, locates the text at the intersection of racism, colonialism, and sexual inequality and sees in Aziz the feminized and colonized object. Frances Restuccia shows how Forster attacks precisely those aspects of language and society that oppress women as well as construct empire. Jenny Sharpe argues that *A Passage to India* "contends with a discourse of power capable of reducing anticolonial struggle to the pathological lust of dark-skinned men for white women" (42).

Bonnie Finkelstein's *Forster's Women: Eternal Differences* (1975) was the first to raise feminist issues in a sustained way. Unlike several more recent critics, she argued for Forster's intellectual sympathy with feminism and saw Fielding's marriage as aligning him with Mrs. Moore as a redemptive force. However, Elaine Showalter in an article two years later argued that the marriage was a betrayal both of Aziz and of the idea of interracial love as a solution to international conflicts.

In current discussions of *A Passage to India*, sexual and racial politics have replaced rhythm, romance, and irony as the dominant topics, but the break between these two discursive realms is not absolute. Contemporary readings are much more resolutely historicized and theorized than those of even the fairly recent past. Yet certain concerns persist: the relationship between political process and private vision, between power and friendship, and the interrogation of the capacity of language to represent these competing claims, these "conflicting urgencies," in the "echoing, contradictory world" (*PI*, 117).

A READING

5

World and Text

Some Problems of Interpretation

Although widely praised, *A Passage to India* was also criticized for exhibiting two rather contradictory qualities. From a British perspective it was sometimes seen as an anachronistic caricature; from an Indian, especially a Hindu, point of view it was considered by some as misleading and unrepresentative, especially in its use of a Muslim protagonist and in its lack of any mention of Gandhi. Attempting to understand the grounds for such critiques may help identify some of the interpretive issues confronting readers.

One person who read the novel with interest was Edmund Candler, the writer whom Forster had visited on his first trip to India, when Candler was principal of a Bengali college in the Punjab. Candler's *Abdication*, a sequel to his earlier *Siri Ram: Revolutionist* (1912), had been published two years before Forster's novel. Between 1912 and 1922, Candler's views had darkened considerably, the latter text giving up on the idea of empire almost entirely. However, even if his hero can recognize the pernicious effect of the unequal status of the Indian and the English, his retreat to nostalgia finally undermines that recognition. For in his eyes, "there was something fine" about the Anglo-Indians. "They were rooted in their convictions. . . . They had lived clean lives, single-minded, consistent, sane. In all direct personal relations with Indians their influence had been wholesome."[1] Little wonder that Candler expressed reservations about Forster's book. What these must have been are readily deducible from Forster's reply:

28 June, 1924

My dear Candler

I am so glad that you think the book good. You are the first critic of it who *knows* India, and I feared the solecisms and the absurdities a globe-trotter inevitably commits, would have stuck out too much, and made the sum-total unreal. I sent it in some fear and trembling indeed. I must firmly if gaily indicate the gulf between us! We both amuse ourselves by trying to be fair, but there our resemblance ends, for you are in the Club trying to be fair to the poor Indians, and I am with the Indians trying to be fair to the poor Club. By busting our respective selves blue, we arrive at an external similarity, but that's all, and I really don't endorse anything you say in your letter! Anglo-India—and still more Anglo-Indians—bear to my mind the greater share of the blame in this gathering tragedy, and were it my object or duty to distribute marks, I should say so. I have almost always felt miserable in a Club, and almost always felt happy among Indians, and I want to go back among them. They won't like my book, I know, because they don't like fairness; dislike it fundamentally, and here something in my own heart goes out to them again. God preserve us from cricket in Heaven! (Lago and Furbank, 2:62)

Politeness and gratitude for being thought a good writer aside, the gulf between them was indeed immense.

For Forster wrote, or at least tried to write, "with the Indians," looking at the club as if it were some form of alien life, a subject for the anthropologist. One can debate how well he succeeded, whether success was even possible in such terms, whether he did not indeed "betray" his class either from the point of view of the Anglo-Indians, who saw him as a traitor, or from the point of view of present-day postcolonial critics, who want to show the text's complicity with a Western, imperial, colonializing project whatever the author's intentions may have been[2] ("betray" in this sense meaning "to reveal unintentionally"). But whatever position one takes in this debate, including the position that the terms of the debate are inadequate, that the book may not be "about politics" even though it can be read politically, it is still essential to define the position from which Forster wrote and that was emphatically from outside the club and partisan to those deprecatingly (or worse) sneered at within its walls.

It is important as well to underline the point Forster made about "fairness." The novel is not a judicial opinion, carefully weighing the evidence on both sides. It is partial and personal and does not pretend to be otherwise, even as it strives ruefully after that doubtful virtue, fairness. And in this, too, it aligns itself with the Indian position. Forster interestingly dramatizes this idea in a scene after the trial where "what to do about Miss Quested" is the immediate problem (chapter 26). Hamidullah, Fielding, and Adela are all speaking, each at cross-purposes with the other. For Adela "while relieving the oriental mind, . . . had chilled it, with the result that [Hamidullah] could scarcely believe she was sincere, and indeed from his standpoint she was not. For her behaviour rested on cold justice and honesty [read: fairness]; she had felt, while she recanted, no passion of love for those whom she had wronged. Truth is not truth in that exacting land unless there go with it kindness and more kindness and kindness again, unless the Word that was with God also is God" (*PI*, 245).

Forster knew that his trying to be fair to the club was not going to cut much ice with them ("Fair!" they might exclaim) and that he would succeed no better with the Indians. But he had to try; "justice and honesty" required it. Indeed, what keeps Forster's novel perennially interesting derives largely from his attempt to keep those Western virtues intact while mediating them through the heart, even running the risk of being misunderstood on all sides. And misunderstanding is inevitable, as the narrator makes clear when he describes Hamidullah's inability to understand Adela's position: "And the girl's sacrifice—so creditable by Western notions—was rightly rejected, because, though it came from her heart, it did not include her heart" (*PI*, 245). Thus possibly both Hamidullah and Candler would misread the book, but Forster was certainly writing more for the former (inasmuch as one can speak of a character in a fiction being its reader), than for the latter.

The criticism concerning the portrayal of the Indian characters is more complex. Nirad Chaudhuri, as we have seen in chapter 3, argued that Forster's choice of a Muslim central character necessarily gave a distorted view of India and that in doing this, Forster was simply sharing "the liking the British in India had for the Muslims, and the corresponding dislike for the Hindus."[3] In such a reading, of course, Godbole is seen as a clown, and his version of love something to be ridiculed rather than considered seriously. Although it is easy to refute the extreme form of Chaudhuri's criticism, the problem he raises—the degree to which Forster wrote within or against British prejudices and stereotypes—is an important one. Are the scales tipped toward the Muslims or is the overarching view that contains all the characters essentially a Hindu one?

One further question needs to be raised here. It is fairly straightforward, but the answer to it is not. When is the novel set? In what year is the action imagined to be taking place? The most common answer is that the characters are living circa 1912, the time of Forster's first visit, but that the narrator describes and comments on them from the vantage of the second visit in 1921. There are certainly echoes of the recent past in many of the scenes, most notably implicit allusions to the Amritsar Massacre in the response of the British characters to the supposed assault on Adela, and Hindu-Muslim relations are more as they were in 1921 than in 1912. At the same time, the club manners and customs have a somewhat old-fashioned feeling to them, although one should not forget the value of anachronism for the British in exile, who found it useful to cling to outdated formalities as a means of keeping what seemed chaotic and incomprehensible at bay. These explanations lead to a further question: why should the novel's placement in time be ambiguous? For one thing, the blurring of the time frame gave Forster additional fictional space. It also encourages a reading of the novel that is more ethical and metaphysical than historical and political. Although in this chapter I concentrate on the text's relation to its historical materials, what I try to do throughout this reading is show that these are far from mutually exclusive positions.

THE WORLD OF CIVIL STATION AND CLUB

"Our mission is a high and holy mission. We are here to govern India as delegates of a Christian and civilized power. . . . In this task we shall not falter. . . . If you agitate, you will be punished; if

48

you preach sedition, you will be imprisoned; if you assassinate, you will be hanged; if you rise, you will be shot down" (Parry 1972, 27). This statement, from the novel *The Lost Dominion* by Al. Carthill (pen name of B. C. H. Calcraft-Kennedy), published in the same year as Forster's novel, would have received nearly universal assent in the fictional Chandrapore Club. So would a similar though less violent description of British intent from Maud Diver's 1920 novel, *Far to Seek:* "the little concentrated band of British men and women, pursuing their own ends; magnificently unmindful of alien eyes watching, speculating, misunderstanding at every turn; the whole heterogeneous mass drawn and held together by the universal love of hazard and sport, the spirit of competition without strife that is the cornerstone of British character and the British Empire" (Parry 1972, 93).

Indeed this is how Forster's club members saw themselves, magnificent Christian warriors at the outpost of empire, their magnificence, as Diver tellingly implies, a function of their total isolation from those they were there to rule. In the Bridge Party scene in chapter 5, they imagine that they are displaying that magnificence, but they reveal pettiness and stupidity instead. What complicates that scene is the presence of Adela Quested and Mrs. Moore, the new arrivals who are not yet ready to accept the roles they are expected to play. "Fancy inviting guests and not treating them properly," Adela exclaims (*PI,* 46). When Mrs. Moore later describes Adela's reaction to her son, Ronny, his response is "how like a woman to worry over a side issue. . . . We're not out here for the purpose of behaving pleasantly. . . . I am out here to work, mind, to hold this wretched country by force. . . . We're not pleasant in India, and we don't intend to be pleasant. We've something more important to do" (*PI,* 49–50). This petulant litany of self-justification rehearses many of the self-serving cultural myths that Forster's text probes and repudiates. By making Mrs. Moore their somewhat uncomprehending audience, Forster suggests how arbitrary, artificial, and inhuman these myths are.

The repetition of the word "pleasant" is significant; with each utterance it becomes further emptied of whatever fragile meaning it possessed. Mrs. Moore can do no more than repeat the word herself: "The English *are* out here to be pleasant. . . . God has put us on the earth in order to be pleasant to each other" (*PI,* 51). That this view finally fails, both in this conversation and within Mrs. Moore's role in the entire narrative, suggests its insufficiency, though by no means its irrelevance. Social relations may provide an image of political relations, especially in the novel, a form that was for Forster "sogged with humanity" (*AN*, 15), but they are not offered as a substitute for them.

It is nonetheless true that neither the British characters nor the narrator speaks about politics. Those characters who are "in process," that is, who are capable of change (either growth, as in the case of Adela, or collapse, as in the case of Mrs. Moore, or something between the two, as in the case of Fielding), understand their problems in ethical or religious—not political—terms. On the other hand, the Indian characters, Aziz in particular, are aware of the political significance of social gestures. Thus, what the final parting between Aziz and Fielding will enact is the impossibility of adequate social relations without radical political change, not the reverse, as critics have often assumed was Forster's position. However, this is to get ahead of our story. We are still at the club, and the Collector's wife is about to open the Bridge Party.

Mrs. Turton "said a few words of welcome in Urdu. She had learnt the lingo, but only to speak to her servants, so she knew none of the politer forms and of the verbs only the imperative mood" (*PI*, 42). For Mrs. Turton, Urdu is not a language, but a "lingo"; the Indians, even those sufficiently placed socially to receive an invitation, are beneath contempt, certainly beneath the courtesies of language, even the courtesy of assuming they speak a language at all. "You're superior to everyone in India except one or two of the Ranis, and they're on an equality," Mrs. Turton reminds Mrs. Moore before she issues her words of welcome in the imperative mood (*PI*, 42). There is an interesting irony in this insistence on superiority and class, both as it is directed toward the Indians and toward the other English. As most writers on the British in India have observed, those who came out to the colonies lived well above their class. In the words of a novelist in 1913, "everybody in India is, more or less, somebody. It must be a very sad change to go home to England," or of a journalist in 1927, "the status of certain classes of Europeans goes up very considerably when they come to India" (Parry 1972, 34). Their lording it over their "subjects"

becomes the more absurd when those subjects could readily put
the aristocratic pretensions of their "magnificent" hosts to shame.

Mrs. Turton plays the great lady with her fellow English as
well, and Ronny shows his deference to her by a quick recital of
many of the cultural myths that characterize British rule. "Assured
of her approbation" for his observation that "no one who's here
matters; those who matter don't come" (*PI*, 39), he chatters on,
describing the unreliability of the educated class and the virtues of
the peasants and landowners. This myth of the corrupt townsman
(usually but not necessarily Hindu) versus the heroic peasant
(usually Muslim) was one of the most enduring and pernicious of
all, and it occurred over and over in Anglo-Indian writing.

Writing in 1886, a member of the Indian Civil Service characterized "the 'people of India' [as] the dumb toiling millions of peasants" whom he contrasted to "the town bred exotics who are
annually forced through our educational hot-houses" (Wurgaft, 13).
Another civil servant, Michael O'Dwyer, lieutenant governor of the
Punjab from 1913 to 1919 and partly responsible for the Amritsar
Massacre, wrote in his memoirs the year after *A Passage to India*
that the reformers "went astray because they did not understand
the *real India*. They legislated for the English-educated India, a
minority of less than one percent. . . . Meantime the *real India* is
drifting away from the justice and authority to which it was so
securely moored" (Parry 1972, 47).

These are the attitudes Ronny is parroting when he says, "the
cultivator—he's another story. The Pathan [referring to a northern,
Muslim, fair-skinned group]—he's a man if you like. But these
people—don't imagine they're India" (*PI*, 34). In the first scene in
the club (chapter 3), Adela expresses a wish to see "the real India."
What she does not, indeed cannot, realize is that she is not simply
expressing a desire—she is speaking in the code of the colonizer.
For "the real India" was a particularly resonant phrase that signaled the British preference for the Muslim landowner over the
urban Bengali.[4] The phrase that Adela speaks here in her new-
comer's innocence will be radically reinterpreted at the novel's close
when Aziz comes to realize that "this pose of 'seeing India' was only
a form of ruling India" (*PI*, 306). Adela's enterprise is thus doomed
to fail, for the club's version of the real India is a distant fiction, a

way of avoiding those they in fact have to deal with. There is little likelihood that she would see that, or anything real at all.

Forster used the stereotypes and conventions of Anglo-Indian writing satirically: India as a test of British character, the Indians as unruly children in need of a strong paternal hand, and Indians as violent, sensual, licentious. The later scene in the club in chapter 20 after the arrest of Aziz is a brilliant reprise of these themes. The Collector presides, longing "for the good old days when an Englishman could satisfy his own honour and no questions asked afterwards" (*PI*, 183). The little band he addresses sees itself as "an outpost of Empire," and in the "abundant figure and masses of corn-gold hair" of "the wife of a small railway official [who] was generally snubbed" (in normal times she would not presume to enter the club) it sees a symbol of "all that is worth fighting and dying for" (*PI*, 181). She is certainly a more camera-ready symbol than poor Adela, covered with cactus needles, her ears filled with an unremitting echo.

"Women and children" are invoked, the "phrase that exempts the male from sanity when it has been repeated a few times" (*PI*, 183), and as further insinuations are made about Aziz's actions (that he had, for example, "paid a herd of natives to suffocate [Mrs. Moore] in a cave"), the hysteria mounts. "It's not the time for sitting down. It's the time for action. Call in the troops and clear the bazaars" (*PI*, 187). The specific allusion is to the Indian Mutiny ("the unspeakable limit of cynicism, untouched since 1857"), but the more immediate reference is to the 1919 Amritsar Massacre. This becomes clearer later on in the narrative, at the start of the trial: "Why they ought to crawl from here to the caves on their hands and knees whenever an Englishwoman's in sight. . . . We've been far too kind with our Bridge Parties and the rest" (*PI*, 216). Mrs. Turton is here recalling General Dyer's crawling order after the massacre, which certainly marked the end of such social forms.

HINDU AND MUSLIM

From the point of view of the club, the Indians below in the bazaars have little individuality and less humanity. Most Anglo-Indian fiction is written from this perspective. What is remarkable, indeed unique, about Forster's novel is the degree to which it omits the stock situations, stereotypes, and caricatures found in nearly all contemporary Anglo-Indian fiction. There is no Kali worship, no blood-stained altar stone such as one finds in Steel's *The Law of the Threshold*, for example: ". . . the clamour of the vast crowd; a crowd that, ankle-deep in fast-clotting blood, was shouting itself hoarse in praise of the Dread Mother, Kali-ma."[5] For writers like Steel, one might add, this is not simply a lurid backdrop but the opening of a polemic to discredit nationalism by linking it to mindless violence and bloody rites. In one area, however, Forster's novel shares an Anglo-Indian convention: the presence of the theme of sexual violence. But Forster's handling of that convention—as discussed in chapter 8 of this volume—baffles explication, as it both figures and deconstructs the colonial anxiety.

Furthermore, in Forster's novel, there is no praise for the Punjabi figures, neither for the Pathan soldier nor for the British administrator-soldier freed from city restraints to play hero on the frontier. Nor is there any sentimentalization of the "toiling ryot," the idealized peasant on his plot of land. These figures enter only implicitly and satirically, where reference to them marks the moral and intellectual limitations of the chatter at the club. And most important of all, there is no "Babu"—the middle-class, Hindu city dweller who is the satiric butt of much Anglo-Indian writing, most widely known from Kipling's *Kim*.

The British attitude toward this figure was, as critics have often pointed out, deeply paradoxical. They were contemptuous of the middle class that their own rule had created, "dismissed them as Babu Jabberjees, [and] treated this only progressive force in India as their arch enemy, and idolized as the true Indian the worst victims of their own economic policies, namely the Indian peasant."[6] In *Kim* the Babu is a patchwork figure made up of English affectations grafted on a set of Hindu clichés: "Hurree Babu held up his hand to show he was engaged in the prescribed rites that accompany tooth-cleaning among decently bred Bengalis. Then he recited in English an Arya-Somaj prayer of a theistical nature, and stuffed his mouth with pan and betel."[7] The absence of this figure or anyone remotely like him in *A Passage to India* is another indication that Forster is not writing within the framework and assumptions of British prejudices, despite the claims of critics such as Chaudhuri and Shonfield.

But the problem of the relative status of Hindu and Muslim in Forster's text remains. For example, what are the implications of making a Muslim the chief Indian character? What does one make of the absence of any mention of Gandhi? To the first question there is an obvious answer and one less obvious. The Muslims were the group Forster knew best on the day-to-day level important for the novelist; that is, although his characters are imagined fictions they are not stage figures, made up of the accumulated debris of conventions and stock gestures. He could imagine their world because he had entered it and knew its intimacies.

Less obvious is Forster's use of his Muslim protagonist to represent both the political position of that community, particularly that of the separatists of the Muslim Young party, and the pluralist and culturally inclusive position of Gandhi and the Congress party. As Frances Singh has convincingly argued, in Aziz's progress through the novel one sees the full range of Muslim responses, and in the third section, in the Hindu state of Mau, one can see his shift toward a Gandhian "acceptance of indigenous tradition [as] the base for independence."[8] For it is in Hindu Mau that the Muslim Dr. Aziz (who has by then largely rejected most Western medicine) can say, "I am an Indian at last" (293). In his last conversation with Fielding in the final chapter, his vision is emphatically the Gandhian one of communal harmony: "Hindu and Muslim and Sikh and all shall be one" (Singh, 322). Singh concludes that "the creation of this new Indian, Muslim in sensibility, Hindu in political outlook, is Forster's implicit contribution to the national movement" (*PI*, 273).

Thus the answer to the first question suggests that one might want to reexamine the second, concerning Gandhi's absence from the text. Indeed, one can argue that Gandhi is, in fact, an implicit presence there. In *E. M. Forster's India*, G. K. Das shows how many of the novel's details allude to specific events: the Amritsar Massacre, the Khilifat movement, the Non-Cooperation movement that temporarily joined Muslim and Hindu. He sees the arrest of Aziz, for example, in the context of the political arrests of 1921–22, including Gandhi's; in the fact that Aziz has both a Muslim pleader and a Hindu barrister for his defense, he sees a reflection of

Gandhi's defense of the Ali brothers. "When the Ali brothers were arrested for their provocative anti-Government speeches, Gandhi defended them publicly, and himself repeated the speeches as a way of protest against the Government's action" (Das 1977, 61).

Furthermore, much of the text's emphasis on friendship and personal relations is not simply Cambridge liberal humanism exported to Asia but a reflection of Gandhian beliefs as well. For in Gandhi's view, the British were "incompetent to deal with the problems of India—which were not primarily administrative at all, but social and religious."[9] Friendship, too, was a goal for Gandhi: "We desire to live on terms of friendship with Englishmen, but that friendship must be on terms of friendship of equals both in theory and practice" (Das 1985, 2). Such equality can never come about when one group has power over another, a perspective that helps explain the novel's ending, which shows the impossibility of a continued friendship between Aziz and Fielding.

There are numerous other allusions that locate the novel politically. We have already discussed the references to Amritsar. At the trial itself, there is an implicit reference to the Rowlatt Acts in the discussion over whether Mrs. Moore's "evidence" is admissible, the witness herself being absent. As several critics have observed, one moment at the end of the trial can serve as a fitting emblem of the tenuous Muslim/Hindu entente that marked the Non-Cooperation movement. The Hindu magistrate, Mr. Das, asks Aziz to contribute a poem for his brother-in-law's magazine:

"I will write him the best I can, but I thought your magazine was for Hindus."

"It is not for Hindus, but Indians generally," he said timidly.

"There is no such person in existence as the general Indian."

"There was not, but there may be when you have written a poem. You are our hero; the whole city is behind you irrespective of creed."

"I know, but will it last?"

"I fear not," said Das, who had much mental clearness. "And for that reason, if I may say so, do not introduce too many Persian expressions into the poem, and not too much about the bulbul [the nightingale, a staple Aziz's poetry]."

. . . .

> "I know you bear me a grudge for trying that case," said [Das], stretching out his hand impulsively. "You are so kind and friendly, but always I detect irony beneath your manner."
>
> "No, no, what nonsense!" protested Aziz. They shook hands, in a half-embrace that typified the entente. (*PI*, 266–67)

That half-embrace between Hindu and Muslim is a wonderfully apt emblem of the entente, but so is the conversation as a whole, as each delicately skirts the sensibilies of the other in an uneasy search for a common ground of understanding. One might note—in connection with my earlier comment that over the course of the novel Aziz moves toward Gandhi's position—that here Aziz still doubts the possibility, which Mr. Das suggests, of the "general Indian," the idea he comes to advocate at the novel's close.

One could argue that while writing his novel, Forster had himself arrived at that part of the Gandhian position that saw communal harmony and self-realization as necessary first steps toward political independence. But he seemed not to want to name that position or explore its consequences in fiction. He was certainly anti-imperialist in his views throughout this period, but as suggested earlier, these views were complicated by his sense that British withdrawal might produce political and social disaster. Forster was well aware of the Non-Cooperation movement and the increasing political agitation during his second visit, but he was protected from it in the very pro-British atmosphere of the Dewas court. The crowds in their Gandhi caps, as he described them in his letters in *The Hill of Devi*, were observed at a distance.

Gandhi was an important figure throughout this period, although his political radicalism developed only gradually. Indeed *Hind Swaraj* (1909), written when he was in South Africa, argued for *swaraj*, that is, self-government, within the framework of the British Empire. That Gandhi's name is never mentioned in the novel may be explicable in part by Forster's intentional vagueness about the time setting, his not wanting to link a particular position with a specific date. This imprecision, however, was also a direct consequence of his belief that "the book is not really about politics. . . . It's about something wider than politics, about the search of the human race for a more lasting home, about the universe as embodied in the Indian earth and the Indian sky."[10] Thus actual events and issues only enter the text metaphorically (the half-embrace) or allusively (Dyer's "crawling order"). They give texture to the narrative, but Forster does not allow them to locate and hence possibly limit it.

However, as recent postcolonial critics have argued, what was for Forster largely an aesthetic choice certainly carries ideological implications along with it. Following this argument, one might want to investigate, for example, what happens to the East, the Oriental Other, when the Western writer makes it an emblem of his own metaphysical concerns. Does this involve the erasure of the Other? Is this a metaphysical version of economic imperialism? Forster, in my reading, is finally too elusive and too skeptical a writer to be explained adequately in such terms. But these remain useful questions insofar as they illuminate certain irreconcilable elements at the heart of his undertaking, as well as the ongoing critical debates in response to them.

MOSQUE, CAVES, TEMPLE

The three divisions of the novel—"Mosque," "Caves," "Temple"—both point to and stand for a range of meanings from the literal to the symbolic. In the author's note to the 1942 Everyman edition, Forster explained them thus: "The three sections into which it is divided, Mosque, Caves, Temple, also represent the three seasons of the Cold Weather, the Hot Weather, and the Rains which divide the Indian year" (*Ab. PI*, 346)—that is, spring, summer, and autumn. They also divide the world into Muslim, British, and Hindu, although the central section is only British in the sense that the British courtroom attempts (and finally fails) to bring to light what happened in the Caves, a geological/geographical site far older than Hindu, Muslim, or British—indeed, "older than anything in the world" (*PI*, 123).

Critics have offered a variety of "translations" of the three divisions: earth, air, water; emotion, intellect, love; reason, form, sense; thesis, antithesis, synthesis.[11] Wilfred Stone has followed the symbolic implications of the triadic organization further than most critics, particularly concentrating on the trinity of sky, water, earth and on the three parts "that Sankhya philosophy [one of the original systems of Hindu thought] assigned to the mother archetype, which are usually translated as goodness, passion, darkness" (Stone, 312). In Stone's readings, the divisions do not correspond in any one-to-one fashion to the elements or emotions he examines: for example, "the Marabar Caves are dry, but in their very rocks are reflections of the primal moistness" (Stone, 313). Thus while sky, water, earth may designate the three sections, all the elements are present in varying degrees in each, for "the theme which this book hammers home is that, for all our differences, we are in fact one. . . . Not only are we related, each to each, as persons, but we partake also of the earth, sky, and water" (Stone, 339). Stone is a subtle and persuasive critic, and in his insistence on unity he strikes a very Forsterian note. But his argument demands that "one read the book in terms of its metaphysics and symbols," not its politics: "one of the aims of the book is to make people and their politics look small" (Stone, 316). I question the usefulness of this distinction, even if Forster's own retrospective view of his accomplishment would seem to favor a symbolic reading, as in the passage already quoted from "Three Countries." There he spoke of "the universe as embodied in the Indian earth and the Indian sky," and further, in describing the novel as "philosophic and poetic," he pointed out "the horror lurking in the Marabar Caves and the release symbolized by the birth of Krishna" (*PI*, 298). Nonetheless, as he wrote elsewhere, "the political side was something I wanted to get in."

A political reading can work directly with a symbolic or metaphysical one. Furthermore, one need not restrict the range of symbolic interpretations. Some of these may have a more immediate resonance than others; probably all are provisional. They enable the reading process insofar as they place temporary boundaries on the indeterminate. As readers of Forster's text, we are asked to make sense of the incomprehensible, to impose order on chaos. The narrator claims that India is finally unknowable, that nothing is what it seems to be. At the same time his text gives narrative coherence to that putative incoherence, through a complex rhythmic pattern of tripling and doubling, repetition and echo—what E. K. Brown, following Forster's own discussion of rhythm in *Aspects of the Novel*, described as its "rhythmic rise-fall-rise."[12] Yet one might argue that the will to order, what can be described as the text's modernist impulse, exists in tension with a countervailing force that would unravel all certainties. From this point of view, one would have to add a final "fall" to Brown's sequence and suggest that even if the design reaches toward synthesis, its components remain antithetical to the last. Thus, the birth of Krishna as described in the final section may bring release but it cannot accommodate and resolve all the tensions—political, social, sexual, and metaphysical—that have built up through the text. Nor need it do so. The novel is far larger than its design, as intricate, complex, and aesthetically satisfying as that is. Like Mr. Das, the magistrate at the trial of Aziz, Forster "had much mental clearness." It is that clarity that makes the text an interrogation, not a declaration, of belief. There are many more questions than answers.

THE TITLE

In his "Programme Note" to Santha Rama Rau's adaptation of the novel for the stage, Forster wrote: "Taking my title from a poem of Walt Whitman's[,] I tried to indicate the human predicament in a universe which is not, so far, comprehensible to our minds" (*Ab. PI*, 328). Forster's mode of exploring that predicament was certainly far more tentative than Whitman's oceanic optimism with its vision of "Europe to Asia, Africa join'd . . . As brides and bridegrooms hand in hand."[13] For Forster as for Whitman the marriage metaphor functioned on both the political and personal levels, but in Forster's case with a more unsettling ambiguity. It was the opening of the Suez Canal in 1869 that generated much of the optimism in Whitman's poem, but in Forster's text that optimism is treated at the very least ironically, for there Suez marks the break between East and West; beyond it, Mrs. Moore's spirit cannot pass. It marks, as well, Adela's retreat from India (no brides or bridegrooms there), a scene given a particularly comic spin in the American missionary's fatuous discourse about East and West and sausages at the statue of de Lesseps at Port Said (*PI*, 266).

Forster also took from Whitman's poem its expansive and exploratory spirit—"For we are bound where mariner has not yet dared to go, / And we will risk the ship, ourselves and all" (ll.

250–51). It was very much in that spirit that Forster wrote to Josie Darling (Malcolm Darling's wife) from Egypt in 1915: "England in these days seems tighter and tinier and shinier than ever—a very precious little party, I don't doubt, but most insistently an island, and there are times when one longs to spread over continents."[14] Nine years later, that Whitmanic longing remained in the completed text, but there it was complicated and ironized. It was no "little bridge of sympathy between East and West" (the phrase previously noted in Forster's 27 September 1922 letter to Masood) that *A Passage to India* constructed, as both East and West were quick to point out, but something possibly more enduring than engineering.

6

Beginnings

The novel begins on an aside, marking an exception: "Except for the Marabar Caves—and they are twenty miles off—the city of Chandrapore presents nothing extraordinary." What is placed outside and yet called into play by this structure of exclusion is the extraordinary. It is a typically oblique Forsterian beginning, holding in abeyance something that will have to be penetrated, gotten to, but "not yet," "not there" (to use the words that close the novel). The syntax of the first sentence grants the Marabar Caves extraordinary status even as it withholds that status from the city, the description of which is the business of both paragraph and chapter.

"Nothing extraordinary" is a combination of words that will resonate singly and together throughout; an apparent contradiction, the words seem to cancel each other out. Yet, as we will see, the "nothing" that characterizes the caves—"nothing attaches to them"—is indeed their most extraordinary feature. But here in the first paragraph the extraordinary is kept out of view and nothing—no bathing steps, no river front, no painting—is a negative out of which the city—rotting, falling, yet indestructible—emerges. It is a description composed on the long view that takes in centuries as well as distance and that mixes the animate and inanimate, rendering the place and its inhabitants as barely distinguishable: "The very wood seems made of mud, the inhabitants of mud moving."

The second paragraph of this four-paragraph chapter has a much closer focus. Indeed, it sounds at the start like a guidebook, identifying the chief structures of the city and suggesting social discriminations as well. The houses belonging to the Eurasians are located on higher ground than hospital, maidan (a combination of village green and playing field), or railroad station. On the highest ground of all is the civil station of the ruling English. From that vantage, the scene recomposes itself as romantic and beautiful: "It is a tropical plesaunce washed by a noble river." The trees, screening out the real city, thus "glorify [it] to the English people who inhabit the rise." But the trees are an ambiguous image. They enable that self-glorifying fiction, yet they also offer a protection to the people below. At the same time they have a vitality of their own: "They soar above the lower deposit, to greet one another with branches and beckoning leaves, and to build a city for the birds." Between that soaring energy and the "overarching sky" that concludes the paragraph, the civil station with all its roads at right angles and its sensible plan of club, grocery, and cemetery becomes an even more diminished thing.

One of the central conflicts of the novel is suggested here almost geometrically in the figure of the right angle and the arch. But if the imaginative sympathy of the novel is invested in the vision of the arch, of the intuitive, of that which sings, it by no means offers this as a consoling vision, on either the physical or the metaphysical, the social or the political, plane. "The sky settles everything," the line that opens the last paragraph of this chapter, leaves very little room for human intervention. The only natural force to challenge it—though expressed in a defiantly human image—is the "fists and fingers [of] the Marabar Hills, containing the extraordinary caves." Thus the chapter ends with a rephrasing of its opening sentence but now not as exception—rather, as that point on the horizon toward which the novel irresistibly and ominously will move.

This first chapter has something of the linguistic and semantic structure of a poem. Each paragraph is like a stanza with the sentences constructed in rhythmic patterns of long and short, often of Biblical parallels, antitheses, and echoes. Of the civil station, for example, Forster writes: "It charms not, neither does it repel." (An allusion to "They sow not, neither do they reap . . . they toil not, neither do they spin" [Matthew 6:26, 28].) As one notes the allusion, one tries to make it work. It is at the very least ironic, for Matthew's fowls of the air and lilies of the field—part of Christ's discourse on the impossibility of serving both God and Mammon—are hardly models for the rulers of Chandrapore. Still, it is a text the British must have invoked often of a Sunday morning, complacently unaware of its potential commentary on their lives.

Reading a novel as if it were a lyric poem obviously is not a strategy that can be sustained throughout the text. Novel reading is much more linear, more forward-driven than the reading of a poem. Indeed, the very next chapter with its competing voices, its rapid population of a heretofore empty stage, requires a very different kind of reading. We now become more like spectators at a play, wanting to learn quickly about those characters who are busy speaking to one another and whom we "accidentally" overhear. But even if the large and sweeping setting of the opening seems far away from the particularized social discriminations that follow, one distinguishes those voices better—is better able to hear what they are saying below their words—if one allows that opening music to sound. Reading prose as if it were poetry is one way of listening to that music.

The music analogy can be made even more precise, for a Forster text has something of the character of an opera. His style, wrote Peter Burra in his introduction to the 1942 Everyman edition, "carries the sort of declamatory conviction that good opera carries" (*Ab. PI*, 318). The set pieces of description function like operatic overtures and like the orchestral interludes that set the scenes. The plots, too, depend on an operatic tension between the extravagant and mythological and the domestic and naturalistic. Forster sometimes has been criticized for not being certain about what effect he was aiming at. What I hope to show is the contrary, that his descriptive flights and riffs, his sudden entry into the scene to set the music going is a calculated, characteristic, and original aspect of his fiction and provides both accompaniment and counterpoint to the social and political tragedy (and comedy) that fill his pages.

Two quite different stories are implied in the first three chapters. One involves the Indians' perception of their rulers, their sense of grievance at those Turtons and Burtons who need only a few months in India to insult and demean them. The second promises to be the colonial variation of a marriage fiction. In the first story, Dr. Aziz is the central character, and his depression on entering the civil station at the sudden summons of Major Callendar aligns the reader with his view: "Depression suddenly seized him. The roads, named after victorious generals and intersecting at right angles, were symbolic of the net Great Britain had thrown over India" (*PI*, 16). In the second story, Adela Quested comes to India to observe her intended, Ronny Heaslop, at work in the Indian Civil Service. There may be obstacles and misunderstandings to overcome, but the expectation is that the plot will be concerned with their coming together. However, what is odd about this second story is that from the start it exists entirely in terms of the first. The obstacles to marriage such as they are seem to have very little to do with the desires or even the individual natures of Ronny and Adela but rather identify something outside of themselves. There is "something hostile in that soil" (*PI*, 18) the narrator observes and it is that hostility that entraps them—that and the nets the rulers cast, which catch them as well as those they rule.

The two stories are linked at the outset in the encounter between Aziz and Mrs. Moore in the mosque. It is a scene that takes on emblematic status as it is reread and revised in subsequent scenes. Aziz comes to the mosque after his rebuff at the club, "the inevitable snub—his bow ignored, his carriage taken" (*PI*, 17) and no Major Callendar despite the summons. "To shake the dust of Anglo-India off his feet! To escape from the net and be back among manners and gestures that he knew!" (*PI*, 18)—this is the impulse that takes him to the mosque, but it is also what propels him through the fiction and what is indeed confirmed, although in ways not yet imaginable, at the close. Ironically, though, it is the meeting in the mosque that most entangles him in that net, even if it seems to promise something quite different, a "secret understanding of the heart" (*PI*, 20)—the words inscribed on the tomb of a Deccan King that Aziz had found so moving he wished them inscribed on his own.

The scene enacts both a clash of cultures and the terms for their possible reconciliation. Mrs. Moore's remark concerning the fact that she had removed her shoes on entering the mosque even though no one else was there to see—"That makes no difference. God is here" (*PI*, 20), she says—has its parallel at the close of the scene. There Aziz says, "Then you are an Oriental" (*PI*, 23) in response to her acknowledging that though she doesn't understand people, she does know whether she likes or dislikes them. The secret understanding of the heart that Aziz longs for seems suddenly realized even if the image is somewhat incongruous—the white-haired, red-faced old lady, mother of Ronny Heaslop, the red-nosed and rude city magistrate, who is the focus of the angry conversation of Aziz and his friends at the start of the chapter, and the "daintily put together," excitable, and indignant doctor who recognizes in her an intuitive sympathy both to him and to his world. The result is that his first representation of himself—aggrieved, indignant, exaggerating—is modified by this sympathy, so that when he escorts her back to the club and she naively wishes that she were a member so she could invite him in, his response is not to complain, denounce, and deride, but to say simply, "Indians are not allowed into the Chandrapore Club even as guests" (*PI*, 23). With this momentary reconciliation, the long view of the opening chapter returns. But it serves now only to emphasize how temporary and inherently unstable are the positions of ruler and ruled: "What did it matter," Aziz mused walking home, "if a few flabby Hindus had preceded him there, and a few chilly English succeeded?" (*PI*, 23).

So soon as this encounter, however, is submitted to the light and logic of the club, it becomes open to quite different readings, both ethical and political. The conversation in which Ronny gradually discovers that the nice doctor his mother has been speaking of is a native and that her voice hasn't disclosed that necessary information reveals with irony and precision the psychology of colonial rule. Ronny is after all perfectly correct to assume impudence in Aziz's voice when he called to Mrs. Moore about her shoes. It *was* intended as impudence, as challenge, and only became something else because the two actors in the scene discovered that they had no roles to play in each other's company. Insofar as Mrs. Moore refuses to register the colonial difference, either with Aziz or with her son, she seems to offer the possibility for transcending it. She reveals the emptiness, the purely mimic nature of the official language and all actions based on it, both as she is able to speak to Aziz and as she can detect the secondhand in the language of her son. But it is a knowledge that has no effect; if anything, it leads at once to compromise. For in order to prevent Ronny from reporting Aziz's words to Major Callendar, she must promise in her turn not to talk of Aziz to Adela, for Adela might "begin wondering whether we treat the natives properly, and all that sort of nonsense" (*PI*, 34). Thus from the start the marriage plot is situated within the colonial plot: the relationship of the "lovers" is primarily a means for depicting the relationship between ruler and ruled.

Whatever illumination occurred in the moonlit mosque remains essentially private for both participants. Later, in going over the scene in her mind, she sees it for the moment as her son saw it, but only as true in outline, not true in fact: "Yes, it was all true, but how false as a summary of the man; the essential life of him had been slain" (*PI*, 34). Yet it is not a knowledge that she can do anything with. The narrator moves from this realization to the final image of a wasp on a coat peg—again, as in the close of the previous chapter, returning to the long view of time and history. The wasp, like other Indian animals, has no "sense of an interior. Bats, rats, birds, insects, will as soon nest inside a house as out; it is to them a normal growth of the eternal jungle, which alternately produces houses trees, houses trees" (*PI*, 35).

The English try insistently to close out that alien world of shifting, indeterminate boundaries. Their life in India is an almost comic replica of their life at home—the same food, drink, entertainment. It is significant that Mrs. Moore has her encounter in the mosque because she feels too closed in by the club (an interesting foreshadowing of the later, crucial experience in the caves). She is bored by the hearty production of *Cousin Kate*, a third-rate play that she had already seen in London, and she is hot, since the "windows were barred, lest the servants should see their memsahibs acting" (*PI*, 24).

But how to break out of that enclosure, how to see India, the "real India" in Adela's earnest phrase, in which (as mentioned before) she echoes the language of the ruler, unaware of the connotations that language carries. "Try seeing Indians" Fielding responds as he passes by (*PI*, 26), thus entering the fiction obliquely, parenthetically, not to surface again for a few chapters. But seeing Indians may also be an empty and patronizing gesture (the Bridge Party that follows this scene is its obvious parody), especially if there is neither equality nor sympathy. It thus may not necessarily be very different in kind from the sneering superiority of those club members who say, "As if one could avoid seeing them" (*PI*, 26) or "why, the kindest thing one can do to a native is to let him die" (*PI*,

27). We are positioned as readers to reject this smug racism insofar as we are able to read through its coded language and convention-alized gestures. Yet we are given no secure vantage from which to do this, since no alternative gestures or ways of behaving seem readily available in the enclosed world of the club.

But the outside world seems dangerous, too—snakes and crocodiles and fields of darkness. As Ronny and Adela and Mrs. Moore return from the club they are diverted by the radiance of the moonlight on the Ganges. Mrs. Moore's response to Ronny's talk of crocodiles in the river—"what a terrible river! what a wonderful river!" (*PI*, 32)—provides not only an accurate register of the double-ness of that experience but also a model for responding to the uncertainties and ambiguities that surround all the major events of the novel. Furthermore, it suggests why the talk between mother and son that follows will fail, as we have already seen in their impasse over the word "pleasant." For Mrs. Moore has "tried seeing Indians," but the event cannot resolve itself into a single meaning. Depending on how you look at it, she finds, the incident changes: "Yes, it could be worked into quite an unpleasant scene" (*PI*, 34). But even if "the secret understanding of the heart" that she momentarily found there is reduced at the chapter's end to the sleeping wasp on the coat peg (an image, like the encounter itself, that continues to reverberate throughout the novel), that sympathy, that ability to see the wasp not as an intruder, but as a "pretty dear," sets her in absolute opposition to her son and his official certainty that "nothing's private in India" (*PI*, 33). Indeed, one could argue that confronting and testing that claim are, in one reading at least, precisely what *A Passage to India* is "about."

"About" is probably the trickiest word in the whole critical lexi-con, although it rarely makes it into such compendia, as it seems so prepositional and innocent. Yet like the pin of the entomologist, it tends to fix the text, and what was wriggling and breathing before becomes suddenly silent and rigid. Is *A Passage to India* about pol-itics or about friendship, about the British in India or the meta-physical discomfort of the Westerner under that enormous and pitiless sky? Is it about persons or ideas, about language or the failure of language? It certainly isn't about marriage, although it borrows some of the conventions of the traditional marriage plot and sets up narrative expectations along its lines.

Even if we move "about" from the level of theme to the level of plot and event, it is not obvious where our emphasis should be. Whose story is it anyway? From whose point of view, in whose interest, do we tell that story? Adela's? Aziz's? Fielding's? Mrs. Moore's? We presume a story in our critical accounts, but we would be hard put to tell that story since, as Borges recognized in his "Pierre Menard, Author of the *Quixote*," the story is consumed in the act of reading, and thus the only retelling possible is an identical word-for-word copy of the original.[1] As soon as we start summarizing we are making critical choices of what to include, what to omit. Therefore, our accounts always presume a partial story that we epitomize through a selection of incidents and characters that will illustrate it best. As Kenneth Burke has shown, very different novels emerge as epitomized through Adela and Mrs. Moore[2]: the former character is fair, careful, unimaginative; the latter intuitive, religious, mythological. Similarly, Malcolm Bradbury distinguished between the "linear social plot," which he read as essentially Adela's story, and the verbal or symbolist plot.[3] Bradbury's distinction follows Lionel Trilling's account of the different functions of plot and story in the novel. "The story," Trilling argued, "is beneath and above the plot and continues beyond it in time. . . . It is greater than the plot and contains it. . . . The characters are of sufficient size for the plot; they are not large enough for the story—and that indeed is the point of the story" (Trilling, 147). In Bradbury's account the verbal or symbolist plot is essentially what Trilling meant by story, or what Forster, a few years after the publication of *A Passage to India*, in the lectures that later became *Aspects of the Novel*, called "song."

The distinction that Forster made there is a useful one for our purposes. It serves to return us to some of the questions that I raised at the start of the chapter, particularly those concerning the problem of developing a decorum for reading Forster's text, of negotiating the lyric and the dramatic, the metaphysical and the realistic, levels of the novel. Song is associated with prophecy in Forster's anatomy of the novel, with the mode of imagining that while "spasmodically realistic" is always in danger of smashing the furniture: "The singer does not always have room for his gestures, the tables and chairs [that is, the stage props of the realistic novel] get broken" (*AN*, 86). There are not too many examples; he can find only four novelists to illustrate the mode of prophecy—Dostoyevski, Melville, D. H. Lawrence, Emily Brontë. It is a quality different from philosophical or poetic reflection such as one finds in Hardy or Conrad: "A prophet does not reflect," nor need he, properly speaking, say anything. Rather "he proposes to sing, and the strangeness of song arising in the halls of fiction is bound to give us a shock" (*AN*, 86). Thus about *Moby-Dick*, for example, "as soon as we catch the song in it, it grows difficult and immensely important. . . . Nothing can be stated about [it] except that it is a contest. The rest is song" (*AN*, 95–97).

As critical discourse this is quite metaphoric or prophetic itself, but it does identify a type of reading experience. Of course we can reply that one can say many more things about *Moby-Dick* than that it is a contest and that these are not irrelevant or incidental observations and may in fact be as essential as its song. But "song" remains in the sense suggested by Forster when, writing of *Wuthering Heights*, he says that "what is implied is more important to [Brontë] than what is said" (*AN*, 100). The degree to which song is fundamental to *A Passage to India* is an issue that is worth considering. One may note, too, that a number of critics have compared Forster's novel to Melville's, particularly in terms of the reader's interpretive quandary, that is, the often baffled attempt either to fathom or to confer meaning on the text.[4]

In any act of critical reading one must decide what issues to bring to the foreground, what patterns, episodes, and characters in the text to isolate and examine, and what to omit. The problem becomes acute in *A Passage to India*, where omission and inclusion are as much thematic as narrative issues. Early in the novel, for example, in the short chapter (chapter 4) that links the first set of scenes with the Bridge Party discussed previously, the narrator moves from describing the social implications of the issuing of invitations for that event to a consideration of the meaning of the idea of invitation precisely in terms of the motifs of omission and inclusion. In a narrative move entirely characteristic of Forster, the fictional material is reexamined to probe for the metaphor, the "meaning" that the social gesture carries. Here the narrator imagines the actual path of the Collector's invitation, following it down the social scale past its last recipient to "humanity grading and drifting beyond the educated vision, until no earthly invitation can embrace it" (*PI*, 37). It is the kind of passage that carries the text's music in a riff or cadenza that blurs the boundary between poetry and prose:

> All invitations must proceed from heaven perhaps; perhaps it is futile for men to initiate their own unity, they do but widen the gulfs between them by the attempt. So at all events thought old Mr. Graysford and young Mr. Sorley, the devoted missionaries who lived out beyond the slaughterhouses, always travelled third on the railways, and never came up to the club. In our Father's house are many mansions, they taught, and there alone will the incompatible multitudes of mankind be welcomed and soothed. Not one shall be turned away by the servants on that verandah, be he black or white, not one shall be kept standing who approaches with a loving heart. And why should the divine hospitality cease here? Consider, with all reverence, the monkeys. May there not be a mansion for monkeys also? Old Mr. Graysford said No, but young Mr. Sorley, who was advanced, said Yes; he saw no reason why monkeys should not have their collateral share of bliss, and he had sympathetic discussions about them with his Hindu friends. And the jackals? Jackals were indeed less to Mr. Sorley's mind, but he admitted that the mercy of God, being infinite, may well embrace all mammals. And the wasps? He became uneasy during the descent to wasps, and was apt to change the conversation. And oranges, cactuses, crystals and mud? and the bacteria inside Mr. Sorley? No, no, this is going too far. We must exclude someone from our gathering, or we shall be left with nothing. (*PI*, 37–38)

We have already encountered the wasp that renders Mr. Sorley uneasy in a context that was similarly "uneasy": " 'Pretty dear,' said Mrs. Moore to the wasp. He did not wake, but her voice floated out, to swell the night's uneasiness" (*PI*, 38). That moment focuses the night's cross-purposes and misunderstandings. Mrs. Moore's ability to acknowledge the wasp, to include it in her sympathy, sets her in contrast to her son who probably would not have even registered it (or if he had, simply would have cleared it off his coat peg). Mrs. Moore's words imply that nothing exists in isolation, that there can be no exclusion, even if powerful political forces would resist this effort.

Since the speech of the characters is for the most part filtered through the narrator's speech, it is often difficult to gauge the authority of an assertion. For example, the narrator in concluding the long passage just quoted seems to allow for a conclusion quite different from Mrs. Moore's: "We must exclude someone," he observes, and we note that within the social relations of Forster's text, it is the missionaries themselves who are excluded; living "out beyond the slaughterhouses," they receive no invitation. In a much later scene, in the aftermath of the trial, the narrator remarks, "How indeed is it possible for one human being to be sorry for all the sadness that meets him on the face of the earth, for the pain that is endured not only by men, but by animals and plants, and perhaps by the stones" (*PI*, 257). In the first scene, the comment is entirely Mrs. Moore's, in the second it is Mr. Sorley's but spoken by the narrator, and in the third it seems to belong solely to the narrator, though it is implicit in the conversation of his characters. Therefore, in order to determine the authority of any statement, we must examine the distinction between seeing and speaking, between vision and voice. Such issues are both technical and thematic, having to do with how the fiction gets told and what it is telling.

7

Narration and Language

WHO SPEAKS?

"I ask you: did he do it or not? Is that plain? I know he didn't, and from that I start. I mean to get at the true explanation in a couple of days."

    —Fielding

"I think you are asking me whether the individual can commit good actions or evil actions."

    —Godbole

"Say, say, say," said the old lady bitterly. "As if anything can be said."

    —Mrs. Moore

These three utterances point to the basic narrative issues of *A Passage to India*. What happened? What does it mean? Can it be spoken or told? At different points in the narrative, the emphasis will fall on one or another of these questions, allowing one to describe it as detective story, ghost story, comedy of manners, travel narrative, and a philosophic meditation that ends in a silence that defies all attempts to order and explain.

    Who holds these various modes together? Can one identify a consistent position from which the narrator speaks? Is he with Fielding, confident that everything can be explained, or with Mrs. Moore, whose outburst echoes Hamlet's "words, words, words" and with similarly nihilistic effect? Is his a position of authority and control, or is he a shape-shifter taking his identity from the characters whose voices he assumes and whose words he ventriloquizes? And how consistent is his relationship to his characters? One senses a shift of interest over the course of the fiction from Fielding to Aziz. Not only is Fielding a much-diminished character by the end of the novel, but there is no attempt by then to see events from his point of view. His return to India is important primarily as it frames the transformation of Aziz from object of patronage to victim to empowered Indian.

For the purposes of this discussion, I refer as much as possible to "the narrator" instead of to "Forster" in order to keep the focus on the textual situation. Of course, this narrator is within the control of the author; indeed, he acts as his agent. But as a voice within the text, he is part of the design contrived by the author outside it. The narrator has an extensive tonal range; he speaks matter-of-factly, sings, orates, casts doubt, speaks ironically. He takes a stance of omniscience one moment and is quite in the dark the next. In his speculative role he shares some of the characteristics of both Fielding and Godbole; in his ultimate inability to "say" he moves close to the position of Mrs. Moore.

The narrator colors and shapes his narrative, but is he finally responsible for it? He seems rather a polyvocal character, whose varied voices join the multiple voices of the other characters. When Forster, speaking of the problem of "what happened in the caves," said, "I willed my mind to remain a blank," he was saying in effect that he did not allow his narrator to know. That is, not knowing was necessary for the creative process as he later described it, but even more important, it is a characteristic of the fiction itself. Thus the narrator, although he often speaks with considerable authority, does not occupy a position of privilege within the text; possibly he may be as uncertain of the "meaning" of his narrative as any of his readers.

In recent narrative theory, the term "focalization" is used instead of the more familiar "point of view" to clarify the distinction between seeing and telling in the act of narration. For as critics like Gérard Genette, who originated the term, Mieke Bal, and Shlomith Rimmon-Kenan (among others) point out, the angle of vision from which the story is narrated does not necessarily belong to the narrator.[1] Rimmon-Kenan shows, for example, that in narratives that use the " 'third-person centre of consciousness' (James's *The Ambassadors*, Joyce's *Portrait of an Artist*), the centre of consciousness (or 'reflector') is the focalizer, while the user of the third person is the narrator."[2] In other third-person narratives, according to this theory, narrator and focalizer move so close together that there is no separate focalizer as character within the text. Rimmon-Kenan sees this happening in *A Passage to India*, which she cites as an example of what she calls external focalization, and she points particularly to the panoramic effect of the opening scene (Rimmon-Kenan, 77). But I would suggest that this description holds only for such scenes: chapters 1, 10, and 12, for example. Otherwise the relationship between the one who sees (the focalizer) and the one who tells (the narrator) shifts frequently—at times the narrator maintains the distance of the opening passage, but at others he allows the character's angle of vision to dominate. Tracing that relationship is a useful way of raising interpretive questions. It allows the reader to distinguish between what the characters think, by seeing events unfold from their angles of vision, and what the narrator says—that is, his representation of their vision—and to consider the one in the light of the other. Thus one can identify with greater precision the beliefs, values, and cultural assumptions that inform the text.

A very good example of this process can be found in a scene we have looked at already, the conversation hinging on the word "pleasant" between Mrs. Moore and her son following the Bridge Party. As Ronny speaks, he is scrutinized closely, first by the narrator, then by Mrs. Moore. The narrative technique Forster uses for this is free indirect discourse, by which a character's thought or speech is embedded in the narrator's speech; it is implied rather than quoted or stated. Free indirect discourse creates a dual voice; the narrator joins his voice with his character's while preserving the idiom, tone, and sensibility of the character's speech. This technique shares characteristics with direct discourse (that is, quotation) and with indirect discourse, a form of narration grammatically signaled by "that," where speech is recalled rather than directly presented. Thus, the quotation "we're not out here for the purpose of behaving pleasantly" (*PI*, 49) could have been stated indirectly as "he said that they were not out here for the purpose of behaving pleasantly." In free indirect discourse the passage would have read: "They were not out here for the purpose of behaving pleasantly. . . . They were here to do justice and keep the peace." Forster used indirect discourse relatively infrequently. It is in his handling of free indirect discourse, however, that one can best observe the subtlety and complexity of his narrative.

As the narrator sets up the scene, the speech of the characters is first directly represented as unmediated dialogue:

> "We're not out here for the purpose of behaving pleasantly!"
> "What do you mean?"
> "What I say. We're out here to do justice and keep the peace."

When Ronny finishes speaking, however, the scene is doubly recapitulated. In the first paragraph of the passage that follows we hear Ronny's justifications and evasions as the narrator carries his voice; in the second Mrs. Moore focalizes the scene, with free indirect discourse used here to double and deconstruct her son's speech:

> He spoke sincerely. Every day he worked hard in the court trying to decide which of two untrue accounts was the less untrue, trying to dispense justice fearlessly, to protect the weak against the less weak, the incoherent against the plausible, surrounded by lies and flattery. That morning he had convicted a railway clerk of overcharging pilgrims for their tickets, and a Pathan of attempted rape. He expected no gratitude, no recognition for this, and both clerk and Pathan might appeal, bribe their witnesses more effectually in the interval, and get their sentences reversed. It was his duty. But he did expect sympathy from his own people, and except from new-comers he obtained it. He did think he ought not to be worried about "Bridge Parties" when the day's work was over and he wanted to play tennis with his equals or rest his legs upon a long chair.
>
> He spoke sincerely, but she could have wished with less gusto. How Ronny revelled in the drawbacks of his situation! How he did rub it in that he was not in India to behave pleasantly, and derived positive satisfaction therefrom! He reminded her of his public-school days. The traces of young-man humanitarianism had sloughed off, and he talked like an intelligent and embittered boy. His words without his voice might have impressed her, but when she heard the self-satisfied lilt of them, when she saw the mouth moving so complacently beneath the little red nose, she

felt, quite illogically, that this was not the last word on India. One touch of regret—not the canny substitute but the true regret from the heart—would have made him a different man, and the British Empire a different institution. (*PI*, 50–51)

In the first paragraph, the third-person perspective focuses a first-person consciousness; a silent speech is represented behind the quoted speech, as if Ronny were thinking through his words at the same time as he was arguing with his mother about the irrelevance of being pleasant in India. The narrator accounts for that dialogue by granting Ronny what is essentially an interior monologue of self-justification constructed out of the catchphrases of the sahib—to dispense justice fearlessly, to expect no gratitude or recognition, to do his duty, to expect sympathy, to finish the day with his equals. But those catch phrases collide awkwardly with another set of clichés by which the ruled are characterized by lies, flattery, incoherence, and bribery. The only link is the four-word sentence of officialdom: "It was his duty." It is only the newcomers who do not find this self-evident, who withhold the necessary sympathy, imagining that one ought to "behave pleasantly to Indians." At this point in the passage one notes an interesting shift in the form of the past tense from the earlier "he worked," "he expected" to "he did expect," " he did think," a shift that conveys the underlying petulance of the implied consciousness. This petulance continues to the end of the sentence, the final image suggesting how little aware he is of the way his words provide a caricature of the official at his club playing tennis with his "equals." As the narrator filters these thoughts through his own speech, he traces an ironic trajectory from fearless justice to the comic image of the reclining official, his legs resting on a long chair.

In the first paragraph, the narrator is listening while his character is both thinking and speaking; the reader is positioned to be aware of both processes. In the second, the situation is more complicated, for the narrator is now observing the process at one remove via Mrs. Moore, whose careful listening focalizes the scene. As she listens to her son, it is the voice of the complacent schoolboy to which she attends more than to the words. She intuits the discrepancy between man and task by hearing the difference between voice and words. If for Mrs. Moore, as for most of the Indian characters, the heart must inform the tongue, then the way that Ronny speaks cancels out the supposed sincerity of his words. His mouth moves mechanically; mouth and tongue seem to have no organic connection. In the first paragraph the sincerity with which the narrator credits him is not so much contradicted as rendered irrelevant, but in the second it is immediately qualified: sincerity is defined as self-satisfaction, duty as mere complacency. It is the moral indecency, not the political, that she reacts to; she finds the self-satisfied lilt of his words shocking, rather than the imperialist doctrine those words contain.

From this point of view we are better placed to assess the concluding statement of the passage, which has always been a stumbling block for readers. Insofar as it implies a social rather than a political analysis of the problems of empire, it seems to suggest that imperialism would not be so terrible if only people were nice to each other, a position that is usually attributed to the author and made to constitute the grounds for most critiques of the text's politics. By analyzing the passage in terms of its use of free indirect discourse, however, one has to conclude that what we are being offered is the partial view of a character, not an authorized statement. As focalizer, Mrs. Moore sees her son simultaneously as Indian Civil Service functionary and as public-school boy. What she observes is how little different the colonial official is from the embittered schoolboy and thus how little he is able to tell her about India. "She felt," the concluding predicate of the next-to-last sentence, holds implicitly for the final sentence as well, a perspective that the dialogue immediately following this passage sustains. As she clinks her rings and says, "The English *are* out here to be pleasant," she makes the interior meditation about "one touch of regret" explicit. The question, of course, remains—does the narrator align his point of view with his character's at this moment? There is no textual evidence to allow us to assume that he does, for the narrator who speaks Mrs. Moore's words is not Forster in his own person (as he might be identified in something like the Egypt pamphlet, for example) giving his opinions on empire.

In the subsequent conversation, the narrator mediates the dialogue, quoting directly but then accounting for the responses of the characters. In each of his comments, however, he does no more than make their thoughts audible. It is their speech we hear even when it is not directly quoted, as the ellipsis makes clear a few lines later. Arguing that "the desire to behave pleasantly satisfies God," Mrs. Moore concludes with a quotation from Corinthians. Although the passage is not completed in the text, one assumes that she continues speaking Paul's words, that the ellipsis implies quotation: " 'Though I speak with the tongues of . . .' He waited until she had done, and then said gently, 'I quite see that. I suppose I ought to get off to my files now' " (*PI*, 52). Paul's text fills a narrative gap, but his words are literally under erasure. The attempt to make them visible and audible is part of the central crisis of the novel. But this scene chiefly enacts the failure of these words when Ronny turns to his files, "the conversation [having] become unreal since Christianity had entered it." And Mrs. Moore, who has introduced the subject in the first place, cannot make the words signify anything either: "Mrs. Moore felt that she had made a mistake in mentioning God, . . . he had been constantly in her thoughts since she entered India, though oddly enough he satisfied her less. She must needs pronounce his name frequently, as the greatest she knew, yet she had never found it less efficacious" (*PI*, 52).

Mrs. Moore has acted as the focalizing agent for the entire scene, even though we have been granted access to Ronny's thoughts at the same time. She performs this function nearly each time she appears. Of the other characters, Aziz, Fielding, and Godbole are used as focalizers, but less consistently: Aziz at the opening of the novel and at the end, Fielding intermittently during the trial scene, and Godbole in the opening chapter of the final section, a passage we return to in chapter 10.

However, free indirect discourse, the device that allows the narrator the easiest access to his characters' thoughts, does not necessarily situate the character as focalizer of the scene. More often it is used as a shorthand device that moves the narrative forward by compressing dialogue, catching the tones of the speaker's voice in passing: the Collector, speaking of Ronny "in quiet, decisive tones said much that was flattering. It wasn't that the young man was particularly good at games or the lingo, or that he had much notion of the Law, but—apparently a large but—Ronny was dignified" (*PI*, 25). As we are placed to observe the scene, the so-called flattery is fairly damning criticism. Ignorant of language, law, and even the recreations of the sahib, Ronny has only his dignity to recommend him. But the Collector's implied speech mocks its speaker even more than it caricatures Ronny, as it reveals the former's blithe indifference to qualifications and his contempt for the language of his subjects, which he contemptuously calls "the lingo" (the word reappears, as we have seen in chapter 5, in his wife's speech at the Bridge Party).

We might also recall the passage examined in chapter 6, where the Collector's invitation is ironically examined in the light of those "invitations [that] must proceed from heaven perhaps" (*PI*, 37). Here free indirect discourse plays the two voices of the missionaries off each other in their debate over what, if anything, might be excluded from the bliss and mercy of God. The conclusion of the passage is given to Mr. Sorley, who refuses the logical last step in Mr. Graysford's catalog of descent: "And the bacteria inside Mr. Sorley? No, no, this is going too far. We must exclude someone from our gathering, or we shall be left with nothing" (*PI*, 41). The effect of this last remark is curiously contradictory (why should "all" equal "nothing"?), but it was prepared for by the first sentence of the passage; the word "perhaps" challenging the confident claim of the infinite embrace of God's mercy. Free indirect discourse is a very economical device here, for it allows us to hear an essentially disembodied pair of voices. Direct quotation would have required a more elaborate form of characterization. But since we have no fixed reference for these characters, their words retain a more problematic status than those of characters we know more intimately. The narrator may dissociate himself from their conclusion, but he had arrived at a similar point at the end of the previous paragraph—"humanity grading and drifting beyond the educated vision, until no earthly invitation can embrace it" (*PI*, 37). Perhaps the difference is that in Mr. Sorley's view, "we" do the excluding from God's embrace; for the narrator there are simply limits on human vision and compassion, a point to which we return when we examine a related passage in the aftermath of the trial (*PI*, 247).

There are numerous other examples of Forster's use of this device to construct the narrative through his characters' language. Among its other advantages it allows for a critical perspective without intrusive commentary or moralizing. Immediately following the motor car accident on the Marabar Road, for example, we are given two indirectly presented responses to it. The more lengthy one is that of the Nawab Bahadur, whose "streams of well chosen words"

(*PI*, 94) were meant to express courtesy and good breeding, their content being of little matter: his gratitude to Miss Derek, his willingness to hold a repulsive dog, his anxiety for his grandson. We hear his words at one remove through the narrator's speech. However, it is not the narrator who concludes this scene by saying, for example, "when the Nawab had gone," but rather Ronny: "When this old geyser left them, Ronny made no comment, but talked lightly about polo" (*PI*, 94). By introducing the subsequent scene in Ronny's implied voice ("this old geyser"), the narrator can suggest that voice's limitations and its crudeness without pausing to elaborate the point. Rather, these qualities become absorbed for the moment in the pathetic little mating dance of Ronny and Adela that follows. (Interestingly, Adela does not resist that word; indeed, their engagement is resumed in the same paragraph, and a short while later she can herself refer to the Nawab as "our old gentleman of the car . . . her negligent tone . . . exactly what [Ronny] desired," evidence of how quickly, even if accidentally, she has assumed the role of Anglo-Indian (*PI*, 96).

The narrator moves in and out of his characters, sometimes holding them in the long view, sometimes speaking from within their thoughts, recomposing the scene from their angle of vision, and sometimes doing both at once as in the scene of Mrs. Moore's departure from India. The narrator describes the "twilight of the double vision in which so many elderly people are involved . . . a spiritual muddledom . . . for which no high sounding words can be found" in his own voice (*PI*, 207–8), but at the same time he both quotes and paraphrases her thoughts:

What had spoken to her in that scoured-out cavity of the granite? What dwelt in the first of the caves? Something very old and small. Before time, it was before space also. Something snub-nosed, incapable of generosity—the undying worm itself. Since hearing its voice, she had not entertained one large thought, she was actually envious of Adela. All this fuss over a frightened girl! Nothing had happened, "and if it had," she found herself thinking with the cynicism of a withered priestess, "if it had, there are worse evils than love." The unspeakable attempt presented itself to her as love: in a cave, in a church—boum, it amounts to the same. Visions are supposed to entail profundity, but—Wait till you get one, dear reader! The abyss also may be petty, the serpent of eternity made of maggots; her constant thought was: "Less

attention should be paid to my future daughter-in-law and more
to me, there is no sorrow like my sorrow," although when the
attention was paid she rejected it irritably. (*PI*, 208–9)

The rhetoric and the rhythms of the start of the paragraph are the
narrator's, but gradually he assumes her point of view, reaching
direct quotation ("and if it had . . .) through free indirect discourse
("all this fuss . . ."). Thus the sudden turning to the reader ("Wait
till you get one, dear reader") has a startling, even disturbing effect.
So much do we seem to be inside the thoughts of Mrs. Moore that
for a moment it is as if she has addressed us. We reject that possibility, but the sense remains that the narrator has disturbed the
decorum of his narrative.

Why does he intrude so insistently, both challenging the reader
and diminishing his character? For he deprives her of her vision at
the same time as he deprives his own text of its chief symbol. At the
close of the scene, the landscape of coconut palms is personified as
waving farewell as her steamer leaves its anchorage: " 'So you
thought an echo was India; you took the Marabar Caves as final?'
they laughed. 'What have we in common with them, or they with
Asirgarh?' " (*PI*, 210).

That moment of direct address to the reader occurs only here;
possibly it is an artistic error. But it also suggests Forster's essential indifference to prescriptive notions of how a novel ought to be
written. In a 1922 letter to his friend Goldsworthy Lowes Dickinson,
he commented on those constraints in a way that suggests why he
found free indirect discourse so congenial a fictional device: "I am
bored not only by my creative impotence, but by the tiresomeness
and conventionalities of fiction-form: e.g. the convention that one
must view the action through the mind of one of the characters;
and say of the others 'perhaps they thought,' or at all events adopt
their viewpoint for a moment only. If you can pretend you can get
inside one character, why not pretend it about all the characters? I
see why. The illusion of life may vanish, and the creator degenerate
into the showman. Yet some change of the sort must be made"
(Lago and Furbank, 2:26).

To avoid the charge of mere showmanship, he contrived a narrative method in which the thoughts of his characters were embedded in the speculative prose of his narrator. This, too, presented
problems, as he wrote to another friend: "There is a fundamental

defect in the novel—the characters are not sufficiently interesting for the atmosphere. This tempts me to emphasize the atmosphere, and so to produce a meditation rather than a drama" (*Ab. PI*, xvi). Most readers, however, find the meditative, speculative voice that speaks through landscape as well as character to be the novel's singular accomplishment rather than its "fundamental defect."

We have already examined some aspects of this voice as it unfolded the landscape of the opening chapter. It reappears sporadically in asides and in those set pieces of description and commentary that use what I have called the operatic mode. Most of the other descriptive passages belong to one or another of the characters—the mosque as it emerges in Aziz's vision, the Mediterranean as the human norm when it is seen by Fielding with relief after "the monstrous and extraordinary" (*PI*, 282), or the birth of Krishna entirely focalized through Godbole (chapter 33). But chapter 10, one of the descriptive passages belonging to the narrator, stands in a somewhat different relationship to the ongoing narrative than do the other set pieces. It is a meditation on atmosphere, a riff on the heat that both contains and is contained within the conversations that take place on either side of it. It simultaneously breaks up those conversations and makes sense of them. Examining that moment and the surrounding scenes helps one raise questions about language in Forster's text: that is, language as something the characters and narrator talk about, and language as the medium for their speculations.

WORDS AND MEANING

Chapter 10 marks an interval, a space between two stages of a conversation: the first is between Aziz, who is sick in bed, and his friends, including Fielding as the unexpected visitor; the second is between Aziz and Fielding alone, the other friends having departed. Chapter 9, the first stage, is full of misunderstanding, suspicions, rumors. The air in the room is oppressive. As the comforters gather round his bed to parry, manipulate, signal, and incite, Aziz retreats into his quilt, providing a comically accurate image for a form of speech that works against communication and connection. In response to the malicious rumor of Godbole's supposed cholera,

Mr. Syed Mohammed "in his excitement . . . fell into Punjabi (he came from that side) and was unintelligible" (*PI*, 105). This detail makes the reader realize that the language the characters are speaking in this scene is probably Urdu, not English. Also, by underlining linguistic and geographic differences (Chandrapore is in Bengal, on the other side of the country from the Punjab), it further emphasizes the idea of language as a means of separation and division. Only when Aziz, emerging from his quilt, recites a poem, does the air clear: "The silly intrigues, the gossip, the shallow discontent were stilled, while words accepted as immortal filled the indifferent air" (*PI*, 105). It lasts only a moment, the promise of Ghalib's poem that "India was one; Moslem; always had been; an assurance that lasted until they looked out the door" (*PI*, 110). The poetry he speaks cancels divisiveness, not because of what the words say but because of the feeling they communicate in the "indifferent air."

Outside, the indifferent air has become hot, it fills a landscape composed of alien noise and the glare of a sinister sun, as the narrator describes it in chapter 10. The air prevents language from forming. Space is filled with noise—the squeaks of the squirrel, the creaking of the brown birds—and then with something less defined but more oppressively felt: "the space between them and their carriages instead of being empty, was clogged with a medium that pressed against their flesh" (*PI*, 114). With the inarticulate world so close at hand, ready "to resume control as soon as men are tired," it is difficult to attend to the claims of a single wasp, as Mrs. Moore does when she calls it "pretty dear" in the passage that concludes chapter 3 (which also describes the near presence of that inarticulate world where "bats, rats, birds, insects will as soon nest inside a house as out" [*PI*, 35]). From the retrospect of chapter 10 we can better understand the phrase "to swell the night's uneasiness" that we queried in our earlier discussion of that passage. For the angle of vision in chapter 10 is remote, located in the vast, indifferent, natural world against which human difference, human gestures, human values disappear: "It matters so little to the majority of living beings what the minority, that calls itself human, desires or decides" (*PI*, 114).

This external world becomes more ominous as the heat increases, "a vague threat which they called 'the bad weather coming,' " since "April, herald of horrors is at hand" (*PI*, 120). The heat, first mentioned here, will increase as the events of the text accelerate. It provides a counterpoint to and intensification of those events, a textual marker of all that is unknown, uncontrollable: "The annual helter-skelter of April, when irritability and lust spread like a canker" (*PI*, 211); "the heat was claiming its own. Unable to madden, it stupefied" (*PI*, 238). Thus the narrator begins to turn up the textual temperature as the intimacy between Fielding and Aziz begins, but by associating that friendship with the inarticulate and heat-infected world, with the fragility, even the impotence of language, and with the factionalism and suspicion among his characters, he dooms that friendship even as it begins. From the narrator's vantage, the squirrel, the bird, the seven gentlemen waiting for their carriages, and the sun itself are all seen from the same distance and with a similar foreboding. Thus when he returns to his narrative in chapter 11 and resumes the conversation between Fielding and Aziz, that sense of foreboding continues, especially as the conversation centers on the photograph of Aziz's dead wife. Her silent view of the scene confirms our view and, indeed, provides an apt emblem for the reader's experience of the text—"how bewildering she found it, the echoing, contradictory world!" (*PI*, 117).

Each of the words in that sentence repays scrutiny. "Echo" in all its forms occupies the thematic center of the text and illustrates its most conspicuous structural device. It is part of the primary vocabulary, one of a set of repeated words that both carry the values and norms of the novel and account for its aesthetic and imaginative power. One should, however, also pause over the word "contradictory" in the sentence just quoted. For the photograph is itself a figure of contradiction, the dead given voice. But it is a speech that returns her to silence insofar as she looks out on a world that she cannot make sense of or speak in—the more so since as a wife in purdah she was allowed no voice in Aziz's world. She is a ghostly presence in this scene, part of a pattern that aligns her with Mrs. Moore, whose voice also is heard after she withdraws into silence and death.

Thus, as an image neither entirely dead nor alive, neither in purdah nor out, the photograph of Aziz's wife plays contradictory roles in the scene. The primary contradiction is social inasmuch as she both participates in and is silent witness to a process whereby women become items of exchange between men.[3] It is her silence, her objectification (she is only a piece of paper) that creates the terms for male intimacy. Ironically, though, it is an intimate moment that never quite takes: " 'I shall not really be intimate with this fellow,' Fielding thought" (*PI*, 118). Yet the failure of connection is, nonetheless, earnest of connection. By viewing the photograph Fielding has, if only symbolically, stepped behind the purdah and become Aziz's brother. After all, when she was alive, his other friends had seen her:

> "Did she think they were your brothers?"
> "Of course not, but the word exists and is convenient. All men are my brothers, and as soon as one behaves as such he may see my wife."
> "And when the whole world behaves as such, there will be no more purdah?"
> "It is because you can say and feel such a remark as that, that I show you the photograph," said Aziz gravely. (*PI*, 116)

Fielding and Aziz attempt a connection that is finally impossible in the contradictory world they inhabit; history, language, "something racial" (*PI*, 260) all conspire against it. The woman in purdah shadows the scene, a symbolic sacrifice to that failure of connection.

This scene leads us to question the relationship between language and silence in Forster's text. Are they antithetical—the former divisive, the latter standing for that which "reconciles and unites?"[4] Does silence belong to song and thus "to a condition of feeling that is the antithesis of ratiocination and therefore of language?"[5] Certainly language is potentially divisive, but it is also the chief means of staving off the anarchy of the inarticulate world. It stands opposed to noise as much as to silence, and silence, too, may be ominous. The silence that follows Godbole's song to the Krishna who refuses to come offers little comfort. The guests have left Fielding's tea party in confusion and disarray, and the ensuing silence seems to emphasize the absence of divinity: "No ripple disturbed the water, no leaf stirred" (*PI*, 80). More ominous still is the silence that accompanies the procession to the caves, causing "everything [to seem] cut off at its root, and therefore infected with illusion" (*PI*, 140).

As Indian speech is represented in the text, it is closer both to silence and to song than is British speech, but Indian speech is not a single entity. There are, as we have seen, so many languages and, as well, the persistent division between Hindu and Muslim. During Fielding's tea party, which ends in so disquieting a fashion, the narrator not only plays each character off the other but juxtaposes their language systems too: "The dialogue remained light and friendly, and Adela had no conception of the underdrift. She did not know that the comparatively simple mind of the Mohammedan was encountering Ancient Night" (*PI*, 76). Aziz's inability to penetrate Godbole's language ensures his later failure in the caves, a catastrophe in the realm of "ancient night" itself. One might describe Godbole's song that closes the scene as prior to language, "the song of an unknown bird," a maze of noises; at least that is how it sounds to a Western ear—and to the Muslim ear as well.

From Adela's point of view, the conversation is all surface; she has no awareness of, let alone access to, the underdrift. A character like Fielding may have some notion that such a realm exists, but only a dim one. In an early version of the sickroom conversation in chapter 9, for example, Fielding listened to Aziz praise the unattractive Rafi with the sense that "something had gone before he didn't understand."[6] This underdrift identifies a mode of speech in which the words of a conversation are only tenuously connected to a deeper layer. It characterizes the speech of the Indian characters.

The speech of the British, by contrast, with its valuing of accuracy and precision, its interest in definition, and its "objectivity," is often unintelligible to the Indians. In the sickroom conversation, for example, what perplexed them most about Fielding's speech was its trust in language for itself. His words "were too definite and bleak. Unless a sentence paid a few compliments to Justice and Morality in passing, its grammar wounded their ears and paralysed their minds. What they said and what they felt were (except in the case of affection) seldom the same" (*PI*, 112). The contrast between these two ways of seeing and speaking was a recurrent concern in Forster's writing. In his foreword to a 1927 novel, Constance Sitwell's *Flowers and Elephants*, he reiterated the point in a way that is illuminating for his own novel: "To the Westerner . . . a flower is usually a flower, an elephant is an elephant, and a diamond a diamond; objects to the Westerner remain real and separable: they can be understood and described, they can be possessed and sold. . . . [T]o the Indian nothing is real and nothing is separable:

elephants and flowers and diamonds all blend and are part of the veil of illusion which severs unhappy mortals from the truth."[7]

One of the oddities of Forster's undertaking in *A Passage to India* involves his attempt to turn English, the language of definition, of the separable and the real, into a language of underdrift. His British characters do not know how to operate in such a space. They are most at home in the often fruitless attempt to name, as when, for example, Ronny and Adela fail to identify the unknown bird in the scene that follows the disturbing silence at the close of Fielding's tea party: "It was of no importance, yet they would have liked to identify it, it would somehow have solaced their hearts" (*PI*, 85). The narrator, however, especially in his meditative mode, attends to the underdrift of the words. He hears beneath them what "would somehow have solaced their hearts." In that mode, his language can be described as an attempt to "Indianize" English, to have it strain toward the condition of poetry and song, but it does not succeed: "Men yearn for poetry though they may not confess it; they desire that joy shall be graceful, and sorrow august and infinity have a form, and India fails to accommodate them" (*PI*, 211). The motif of yearning and failure is brought to the foreground in the fiction; it may also be a rueful assessment of the narrative project itself. Is the passage to India ever accomplished?

From this point of view the narrator's comment that concludes the scene describing the failure to name the bird is particularly problematic: "But nothing in India is identifiable, the mere asking of a question causes it to disappear or to merge in something else" (*PI*, 86). Is such a statement a version of those despairing, angry words of Mrs. Moore: "Say, say, say, as if anything can be said"? Is it an implicit admission of the possible failure of his own narrative? Or does it position both reader and narrator at a safe distance from the fiction, confident that such confusions could not occur in the familiar English world? Possibly all three questions should be answered in the affirmative even if the third "yes" would seem to contradict the other two. For while one may acknowledge the partial accuracy of the observation that "Forster's writing . . . represents the experience and expectations of a powerful social class," that it rests "upon shared class assumptions,"[8] and that it is therefore protected from the incomprehensible and the illusory, one should also note a contrary tendency, a skepticism about the efficacy of any utterance, Forster's included. Benita Parry's argument that the text "dissects its own informing ideology" (Beer 1985, 30) suggests a resolution to this apparent contradiction, insofar as it implies resistance to a language that was, for Forster, inescapable.

Whatever side one takes in this debate, however, whether one views the author and reader as safely above the fiction or at risk and implicated in it, one must still acknowledge the primacy of the word in Forster's writing. For him the writing process seems to have involved a movement from word to idea. Unlike many writers—George Eliot is a good example, so is Tolstoy—Forster did not write to illustrate an idea, to preach, explain, or convert, but to discover meaning inside language, even if that might lead to the emptying of all language into a self-imploding, self-canceling "boum." Thus it is not so much "collusion" in a civilized critique—in the words of Ebbatson and Neal—that the text demands of its readers as a willingness to interrogate, as the text itself does, one's cultural assumptions and certainties. That tone "of a civilized, literate English observer" (Ebbatson and Neale, 61), which critics like to call Forsterian, more often than not falters or fails when it comes close to the underdrift of language or when it attempts to convey experience seemingly beyond the reach of any linguistic register.

Words matter. One can simply list the key words of the text and recover the novel in epitome: *sky, arch, arching, arcade, echo, echoing, silence, net, dream, ghost, death, heat, darkness, rocks, stones, mud, mystery, muddle, snakes, wasp, song, poetry, kindness, intimate, pleasant, private, nothing, no, not, extraordinary, personal relations, traveling light, to label, friend, brother, come, perhaps.* The words resonate singly and in clusters; they take on different meanings in different situations—the overarching sky and the arcade of the mosque, for example, stand at opposite poles of the textual universe, the one denying, the other affirming the value of human experience. One can trace structural patterns in the repetition of *wasp* and *snake* and follow the echoes of *echo, dreams, silence.* One can set up clusters of words in thematic opposition: *intimate, pleasant, private* against *death, darkness, mystery; personal relations* against *traveling light.* But against all these one must set the one word that tolls most emphatically through the text and is repeated more than any other, *nothing,* the antimatter of the caves and the subject of the next chapter.

8

Caves

The expedition to the caves is the third major episode in the narrative sequence—bridge party, tea party, picnic. All three episodes follow a similar pattern. There is a social occasion bringing together a large group of characters. As the characters group and regroup, attempts at connection are made but something is always slightly awry. Fissures and gaps, the geography of the caves themselves, open in the social words and gestures. It is a type of episode that occurs frequently in the English novel. Jane Austen is probably Forster's model here; her picnic on Box Hill in *Emma* offers a similarly dangerous occasion for mistakes and misunderstandings. Forster had used the device before, particularly in such short stories as "The Curate's Friend" and "The Story of a Panic." In *A Passage to India*, however, where invitation, the Hindu cry "come, come," is as much theme as it is narrative event, the social occasion as transforming moment becomes the organizing principle.

The Marabar Hills, the setting of the third episode, loom over the earlier two as well. As Adela, dissatisfied with the Bridge Party, looks "through a nick in the cactus hedge at the distant Marabar Hills, which had crept near, as was their custom at sunset" (*PI*, 45–46), she encounters Fielding. The result of that talk is his invitation to tea. It is during that second party that Aziz attempts to get Godbole to describe the caves, but runs up against the wall, the "ancient night," of Godbole's mind. Thus when he issues the ill-fated invitation to the caves, he takes on a role that he cannot possibly fulfill, for he knows no more of the caves than his guests do. Yet the gesture is crucial; while making it he is a free man, in possession of his own country, even if that freedom lasts only a moment, to be violently disturbed by the sudden entry of Ronny.

The social relations in each episode are tenuously held together. The scene built around the collar stud illustrates this nicely. Offered by Aziz to Fielding immediately before the tea party begins, the collar stud signals the generous, the impulsive, but also the untrue in the service of friendship—a truth of mood, not a verbal truth, to use the distinction made later in the scene (*PI*, 72). For it is the collar stud he is wearing, not the spare one he claimed to have in his pocket, that Aziz gives to Fielding. But that missing stud is precisely the detail that Ronny registers as index of the Indian's "fundamental slackness," his inability to hold anything together. It thus stands as a figure of the incoherence of the tea party, the impossibility of accurately decoding the other's words and gestures, and a foreshadowing of the disruptions in the picnic to come. As intimacy among the characters increases, so does the potential for disaster.

Aziz's invitation is a "facile remark," language as social gesture. It is meant to cover his embarrassment over his meager house, a place unfit for the entertaining of British ladies. Similarly, when Adela later remarks that she should like to have gone to the Marabar Hills, her words have no meaning. Her language is time filler, a social gesture like Aziz's, now prompted by a picturesque and distant scene. But her words are overheard and become falsely fixed; they are assigned meaning: the ladies are offended; they have expected an invitation daily. Thus nothing becomes a false something in much the same way as the caves themselves will become the site of contested meanings, taking on the history of an event that didn't happen, an event without a name.

But once a name is applied, a meaning falsely fixed, it takes root in the air. As they ride toward the caves, for example, "the withered and twisted stump of a toddy palm" seems to become a venomous black cobra. "When [Adela] looked through Ronny's field glasses, she found it wasn't a snake . . . [but] the villagers contradicted her. She had put the word [snake] into their minds and they refused to abandon it" (*PI*, 140–41). (The field glasses are a nice touch, functioning as both instrument and metaphor. We mistrust them to the degree that we know that we cannot rely on Ronny's vision, that the reality they focus must somehow be less true than the false identification of tree stump as snake. Also as putative weapon they become the chief prop in the narrative of sexual assault and are offered as evidence at the trial, "occular proof" in the words of Othello. But they reveal nothing.) Aziz, too, insists on the mistake, drawing it into the narrative of his hospitality. As he explains it, the snake "had reared himself up to watch the passing of the elephant," that elephant he had obtained through so many favors and arrangements, whose appearance at the station caused him "nearly [to] burst with pride and relief" (*PI*, 138). His vision is no more accurate than the others', and as they approach the caves, an external view that seems, nonetheless, to position them inside the caves, his inability to see ominously foreshadows the events to come: "The plain quietly disappeared, peeled off so to speak, and nothing was to be seen on either side but the granite, very dead and quiet. The sky dominated as usual, but seemed unhealthily near, adhering like a ceiling to the summits of the precipices. . . . Occupied by his own munificence, Aziz noticed nothing" (*PI*, 141). Even before the caves are entered, their presence is rendered in claustrophobic terms. "A horrid, stuffy place, really," observes Mrs. Moore, and this is before her "antivision" in the caves themselves.

Although Aziz is the host, he is the one most at risk in the episode of the caves. The enterprise is fraught with difficulty from the start. The simplest details, the provision of food and drink, assume enormous proportions: "Trouble after trouble encountered him, because he had challenged the spirit of the Indian earth, which tries to keep men in compartments" (*PI*, 127). Much of the accumulating anxiety of the scene is connected to this worry over arrangements and the consequent need to improvise, to rearrange when the unexpected occurs, as happens from the start: Fielding and Godbole miss the train; Mrs. Moore chooses not to go into any more caves. There is no stable moment for Aziz; even the moment of greatest joy, his pleasure in watching Mrs. Moore accept his hospitality, "held the seeds of its own decay" (*PI*, 143). From the start, Aziz attempts to hold the outing together by an ever-increasing hospitality like his hero, the emperor Babur, who "never . . . ceased showing hospitality . . . [and] never in his whole life . . . betray[ed] a friend" (*PI*, 143–44). But the caves resist such human aspirations and feelings, countering them with a terrifying echo, a reductive and monotonous noise, "boum" or "ouboum." On that sound the entire narrative hinges. Once Mrs. Moore hears it, everything unravels; it "began in some indescribable way to undermine her hold on life" (*PI*, 149).

Mrs. Moore's experience is an important preliminary to Adela's. There is an apparent assault, an immediate revulsion, a sense of suffocation, the terrifying echo. In daylight, it is all readily explained. "The vile naked thing that struck her" was only a baby "astride its mother's hip. Nothing evil had been in the cave" (*PI*, 147–48). But the echo, "the overlapping howling noise," the unvarying response to any word or feeling, cannot be shaken or ignored. It undermines her hold on life, it dissolves the support of "poor little talkative Christianity," it renders her a figure of negation, incapable of "communicat[ing] with anyone, not even with God" (*PI*, 157).

Mrs. Moore simply leaves the caves and by that act withdraws from the narrative as well. As her metaphysical horror deepens, she is rendered silent: "Then she was terrified over an area larger than usual; the universe, never comprehensible to her intellect, offered no repose to her soul . . . She lost all interest, even in Aziz, and the affectionate and sincere words that she had spoken to him seemed no longer hers but the air's" (*PI*, 150). Her withdrawal from human contact has a sour and diminished quality to it; the abyss she encounters is "petty, the serpent of eternity made of maggots" (*PI*, 208). The difficulty in interpreting her role, however, arises from the curious fact that the more she denies human contact, even to the degree of seeming to betray Aziz (after all, as her son points out, if she knows his innocence she is obligated to testify for him), the more efficacious she seems to become in the lives of the other characters, as we will see in the trial scene and in the concluding events in Mau.

At the center of the episode are three motifs that are found in much colonial fiction—metaphysical horror, sexual fear, and India as woman[1]—but interrogated and reinterpreted, as each motif is played off against the other. Mrs. Moore's deranging experience in the caves illustrates the first. Adela's experience also illustrates that horror, but her role in the scene is chiefly connected to the motif of sexual fear. In the alleged assault and the club reaction to it we find a paradigm of that fear. However, the motif is developed in a totally unpredictable fashion; indeed, in its drastic revision the boundary between victim and aggressor is blurred. One could argue, for example, that the role of victim in the fiction of sexual assault may possibly belong more to Aziz than to Adela. He is, at least, the character whose sufferings are more permanent, whose life is peremptorily and utterly changed. From this point of view one can speak of Aziz as occupying the textual position of woman, as he is both silenced and violated. In such a position he makes manifest the third motif, the identification of India with the feminine: "India, even to her intimates, seems still a veiled mystery, aloof, yet alluring, like one of her own purdah princesses" (Parry 1972, 97). That was Maud Diver in 1916 using a pervasive metaphor that was still present, even in Indian writing, as late as 1946 in Nehru's reference to India as "shameful and repellent, . . . occasionally perverse and obstinate, sometime even a little hysteric, this lady with a past" (Parry 1972, 68).

All three motifs converge at the central scene. As the narrative reaches its point of crisis, the pace slows. Neither Adela nor Aziz seems aware of the imminent danger as they continue the "slightly tedious expedition." Although they have little to say to one another, that little is potentially dangerous. Their words have a way of not meeting. Earlier, when Aziz was expatiating on his friendship theme, Adela had broken up their conversation by alluding to her marriage, to her Anglo-Indian worries. As they toil up the rocky hillside in the blazing sun, she blunders again, this time with her question about the number of Aziz's wives. In each instance it is Aziz who is thrown off balance by the questions, who has to improvise in order to regain his composure. This is part of a pattern we noticed earlier—always having to fit the unexpected into a preconceived scenario. This pattern has the ironic effect of making his last improvisation, his excusing Adela's sudden absence from the scene after Fielding arrives, seem disingenuous, almost incriminating. The narrator, however, who has aligned his perspective with Aziz's throughout the scene, attempts to mitigate the effect: "He was inaccurate because he desired to honour her, and—facts being entangled—he had to arrange them in her vicinity, as one tidies the ground after extracting a weed" (*PI*, 158). But the anxiety that has built up since the start of the expedition does not dissipate, especially since no one—not the reader, the characters, or, apparently, the narrator—has any idea of what has just transpired.

Thus the inevitable question: what happened in the caves? Although the narrator will not or cannot tell, critics have been busy with solutions, ranging from the physical to the metaphysical, to the psychological: it was Aziz; it was a guard angered that the walls had been scratched and who thus attempted to pull Adela away; it was hallucination; it was projection, that is, sexual desire transformed into sexual outrage; it was "the meeting with oneself . . . the meeting with one's own shadow" (Stone, 335); it was the return of the repressed, a revelation of the inadequacy of the merely rational. All solutions that require another actor—Aziz, a guard, etc. —can be ruled out at once. Aziz is entirely protected by the narrator, who never allows the reader to lose sight of him and who has positioned him throughout the narrative as a figure of loyalty and given him a kind of emblematic status in his speech about the emperor Babur never betraying a friend.[2] The guard theory fails for lack of the slightest intimation of textual evidence. It is also parodied by Hamidullah after the trial when he enters the conversation between Adela and Fielding as they are discussing this possibility: "There are one hundred and seventy million Indians in this notable peninsula, and of course one or other of them entered the cave. Of course some Indian is the culprit" (PI, 253). Hamidullah is, of course, sarcastically parroting the Anglo-Indian point of view, which is rejected definitively, although—and here Forster intensifies the irony—the Anglo-Indians "still believed [Aziz] was guilty, they believed it to the end of their careers" (PI, 243).

All other readings—from metaphysical terror to sexual hallucination—are possible, neither advanced nor ruled out by the narrative. That something horrifying could happen in that space that is at once dead granite and living stone we know from Mrs. Moore; and there is the constant echo. But it is not an experience to which we can give a name. What we are given instead is the intensification of the atmosphere in explicitly sexualized terms. We know that Adela has just faced the absence of love in her prospective marriage, "the discovery had come so suddenly that she felt like a mountaineer whose rope has broken" (PI, 152), oddly foreshadowing the broken strap of the field glasses. We also know that something about the foothold in the rock reminds her of the pattern made by the wheels of the Nawab Bahadur's car in the nighttime trip on the Marabar Road, when their engagement resulted from the collision with the unknown animal—"my hyena," Adela called it. There is also the intensifying heat, although on the train that morning Adela had announced in her "theoretical" fashion, "I don't believe in the Hot Weather. . . . I won't be bottled up" (*PI*, 134). The violent, the animal, the uncanny, the unknown, the hot—these are the qualities that attend Adela's entrance into the bottled-up darkness of the cave. Our sense that something will explode or erupt is carried by the language and the pacing of the scene but in such a way as to prevent our imagining it in any identifiable shape.

The caves as geographical/geological fact have been part of the landscape of the novel from the first sentence, where they stand as the extraordinary exception to everything else beneath the overarching sky. They form part of a landscape of "incredible antiquity." To describe them the narrator has to go back before history, even before "our globe was torn from [the sun's] bosom" (*PI*, 123). They are in Frank Kermode's words "a figure of that place [he is translating Derrida's term, *khora*] always already in place, without dimension or direction, not a realm, not a being present, yet not an absence, the rhythms are the rhythms of negativity itself."[3] Thus positioned, they stand outside of human experience altogether, but, curiously, the "dead granite" from which they are formed is described in persistently anthropomorphic terms. They first appear as fists and fingers, a phrase that is frequently repeated; in chapter 12 they "stand knee deep, throat deep in the advancing soil." Their interior surface is a "skin, finer than any covering acquired by the animals, smoother than windless water, more voluptuous than love" (*PI*, 125). Entrance is through holes and orifices; "the hole belched and humanity returned" (*PI*, 147). But this mimicry of the human ends up by resisting the human, for the caves "bear no relation to anything dreamt or seen." "The usual function of anthropomorphism is to domesticate the non-human into meaning," as Gillian Beer argues, but in Forster's usage it works quite otherwise. "The powers of the human mind and the attempt to perceive all other elements of life in terms of the human creates claustrophobia and oppression."[4]

Although the caves are imagined as "older than all spirit," as prior to language, their interior walls have been polished by human hands. It is significant that the sect they are connected to is the Jain branch of Hinduism. Based on ascetic, animistic principles,

Jainism conceives of all matter as living. Thus the vow of *ahimsa*, harmlessness (nonviolence in Gandhi's terms; he was an adherent of this sect), has profound ethical implications in its abjuring of all injury to living matter, even to stone. The anthropomorphic language that Forster uses possibly has its origin here. Certainly the questioning that runs through Forster's text, of what to include in "our gathering" (*PI*, 38), has a very clear answer in Jain terms—everything. The caves thus mark not so much the nonhuman as the very limit of the human. Indeed, even the contradictory terms of their description—that is, their being described as indescribable—connects them to Jain belief. "Jaina logic admits a . . . judgement of indescribability. . . . In view of the complexity of the objective world, and of man's limited knowledge and imperfect speech, Jaina logic anticipates and admits situations which cannot be described in terms of simple 'yes' or 'no.' "[5]

The caves are an equivocal space. The language that describes them from a distance emphasizes the graceful, the aesthetic, the picturesque; a near view places them outside the reach of such categories with the emphasis on the dark, the empty, on nothing. The unvarying pattern of tunnel, circular chamber, tunnel, circular chamber, the multiplication of empty spaces, yields nothing: "Nothing, nothing attaches to them . . . nothing is inside them . . . if mankind grew curious and excavated, nothing, nothing would be added to the sum of good or evil" (*PI*, 124–25). The reiteration of nothing has an incantatory effect, but it also has the effect of activating nothing, of making it something.[6] One sees this in the frequent negative puns throughout the text, for example: "nothing in India is identifiable" suggests "India is where one can identify nothing," or, paradoxically, "nothing embraces the whole of India" where nothing takes on the meaning of nothingness.[7] Godbole's explanation of the relationship between absence and presence—"absence implies presence, absence is not non-existence" (*PI*, 178)—is a variation on this theme, on the link between nothing and something, the Jain concept of the simultaneity of yes and no. We may say with some confidence that nothing happens in the caves, but that nothing is the central narrative something, the nonevent that reorders all relationships and social and political structures.

The caves were always part of Forster's conception of the novel. When he began it, he later remarked, he "knew that something important happened in the Malabar [*sic*] Caves, and that it would have a central place in the novel—but I didn't know what it would be. . . . The Malabar [*sic*] Caves represented an area in which concentration can take place. A cavity. They were something to focus everything up: they were to engender an event like an egg" (*Paris Review*, 8–9). The egg allusion is interesting; it echoes the description of the Kawa Dol, containing the "bubble-shaped cave that has neither ceiling nor floor, and mirrors its own darkness in every direction infinitely. If the boulder falls and smashes, the cave will smash too—empty as an Easter Egg" (*PI*, 125). What is engendered there is emptiness, the nothing that is so insistently elaborated and "confabulated" through the text. That last curious word, *confabulate* (to talk together), occurs at the crisis, when Aziz discovers that Adela is missing and can neither find her nor "her" cave. The caves all look alike; they seem to proliferate in every direction, to talk among themselves, to tell the tale, but only to each other: "Caves got behind caves or confabulated in pairs" (*PI*, 154). To the questions of Aziz, "which contains my guest? which is the cave I was in myself?" (*PI*, 154), they have no answer. They may be literally the space of story making, of confabulation, but there is no available glossary for their language, that singular sound that reduces all meaning to boum.[8]

All the manuscript evidence suggests that engendering that event was the most difficult part of the writing process. There are numerous versions of each stage of the episode, most of the earlier ones centering more on Adela than the final version does. In one of these, a physical assault occurs, although the identity of the assailant is uncertain. Adela assumes it is Aziz, but all she can see is "an extra darkness [that] showed that someone was following her down the entrance tunnel. . . . She struck out and he got hold of her other hand and forced her against the wall" (*Mss.*, 242–43). This has entirely disappeared from the novel itself, where we never follow Adela into the cave; it is only during the trial and subsequently that we are given any glimpse of that experience from her point of view.

The process of revision raises a series of interpretive questions. What remains of the assault? Does it leave violence and disruption in the text? If Forster had originally used the rape motif in its most culturally determined way—that is, imagining the dark colonial sexually attacking the English woman—does revision eliminate that dimension or merely suppress it? Does substituting the motif of the East as unknowable for the motif of the East as sexually threatening merely replace one colonial myth with another? Does the implicit linkage of racism and rape undermine the anti-imperialist argument carried by the friendship theme? Such questions are worth pursuing; if nothing else, they provide an index for the difficulty of the text, especially the difficulty of making it yield a meaning in any tidy formulation. Furthermore, these questions are, in large measure, inside the text itself, although the vocabulary in which I present them here belongs to current critical discourse. By refusing to stage an assault scene, yet refusing to replace it with any scene at all, and by leaving traces of the original scene in the responses of the other characters, Forster made his own complicity with colonial assumptions his subject. The text thus becomes an interrogation of his use of these cultural assumptions, particularly the assumption that an English woman is at risk in the company of the sexually voracious Oriental. All possibilities are finally left open, even if the careful reader can exclude one or another of them. As Forster wrote in a letter to a friend shortly after the book's publication, "In the cave it is either a man, or the supernatural, or an illusion. If I say, it becomes whatever the answer a different book" (*Ab. PI*, xxvi).

In the letter I have just quoted, Forster explains his reasons for willing his "writing mind . . . to remain a blur." It was necessary to get "the spiritual reverberation going. I call it a 'trick': but 'voluntary surrender to infection' better expresses my state." This is a very suggestive phrase, recalling the unpublished "Kanaya" fragment discussed here in chapter 2 in connection with *The Hill of Devi*. For that memoir is a detailed account of a surrender to lust. Omitted from his letters and from his retrospective re-creation of his stay at Dewas in *The Hill of Devi*, the experience is still silently there in that public narrative. In the private memoir, he described himself at the close of that experience as "disintegrated and inert," having played out a game of sexual politics where the object of desire was "a slave, without rights, and I a despot whom no one could call to account" (*Hill*, 324). The "Kanaya" episode thus reverses the colonial myth of the lascivious Oriental, replacing it with the colonial reality of the lascivious European. It is a moot

100

point whether Forster recognized himself in this role. Possibly what makes the caves episode so baffling is that at its center, too, there is a similar evocation and blocking out of that despotic sexuality, leaving a mystery that is both physical and metaphysical, imagined in a nearly disembodied atmosphere of heat and lust.

The episode ends abruptly. The mystery of Adela's sudden departure is replaced by the mystery of the arrest of Aziz and the inexplicable charge of Adela, "such a dry, sensible girl, and quite without malice: the last person in Chandrapore wrongfully to accuse an Indian" (*PI*, 179) in Fielding's perplexed view. The caves recede; "their nasty little cosmos disappeared, and gave place to the Marabars seen from a distance, finite and rather romantic" (*PI*, 168). But the echo remains.

9

Trials

In contrast to the caves, the courtroom is entirely a human creation; it is the space of logic and language. What happens in the darkness of the former is scrutinized in the light of the latter. It is never really brought to light, however, for even though the courtroom is the domain of the rational, it is not entirely cut off from the mysterious or the magical. The two apparently opposed narrative sites, caves and courtroom, exist in an interestingly parallel and reciprocal relationship with one another.

The narrator focuses on two sets of events as he leads up to the trial: on Fielding's attempts to discover the truth, to organize the defense, to resist the herd mentality of the club; and on Adela's attempts to rid herself of her echo and, like Fielding, to discover the truth as well. Aziz almost entirely disappears from the narrative at this point. Indeed for 10 chapters (17–26) he does not speak except to say twice to Fielding, "You have deserted me." Although this accusation really does not apply to Fielding, who has devoted himself entirely to Aziz's defense, it may describe the narrator, whose interest notably shifts here. It moves from Aziz, the central figure of the previous episode, imagining himself to be the emperor Babur perched on his elephant dispensing hospitality and invitation, to Adela, who, as a result of her experiences, "was no longer examining life, but being examined by it; [who] had become a real person" (*PI*, 244–45). One may ask whether this shift is merely a narrative device that will make the sudden turnabout at the trial the more striking, or whether Forster lost sight of Aziz as a result of his preoccupation with the moral and spiritual testing of Adela.

The simplest formulation of the problem is: Who was on trial? To such a question, one would have to reply, "Adela and, to a lesser degree, Fielding." In this sense, Forster used the trial "in the traditional literary way, as a spiritual test for all the characters in the book."[1] But the trial itself is also important as it both enacts and stands for a Western epistemology and as it points to both the virtues and the limitations of this way of conceiving reality. In the discussion of language in chapter 7 we looked at the contrasting conceptions of language held by the Indian and the British characters as they illustrate Forster's conception of epistemological difference ("objects to the westerner remain real and separable . . . to the Indian nothing is real and nothing is separable" [Foreword to *Flowers*, ii). Accuracy, precision, definition—these qualities, too, are on trial.

But so is Aziz. One result of the shift of focus away from Aziz is that the narrator prevents any questions from being raised about his innocence. Here he aligns himself with the Fielding position that "Aziz *was* innocent, and all action must be based on that" (*PI*, 173). Moreover, one should observe that the judicial process itself obscures Aziz. In the speech of the British characters he is always "the prisoner," or "the defense"; he is effectively deprived of his identity. Indeed the last thing he says before going off to prison at the end of chapter 16 is "my children and my name" (*PI*, 162). From then until the end of the trial he is silent. Presumed guilty, certain to have a trial that will confirm that guilt, he does not exist. Nonetheless, one could argue in terms of a postcolonial critique that the shift from Aziz to Adela is an example of the colonial appropriation of the other, that Aziz's situation is used as the occasion for Adela's spiritual crisis, his own crisis left to be inferred. However, if this is true, it is only so temporarily. By the end of the novel the transformation and empowerment of Aziz are the central issues. Furthermore, it should be pointed out that the comment about Adela's becoming a real person is made through free indirect discourse. It is Fielding, not Forster, who registers this shift. The degree to which the narrator endorses his character's assessment here is open to debate.

In part we watch the events leading up to the trial and the trial itself through Fielding's honest, if limited, vision. However, there is a telling detail at the end of the caves episode that underlines this limitation. The picnic having unraveled, Adela having departed mysteriously, Fielding does his quick bit of tourism: "Fielding ran up to see one cave. He wasn't impressed" (*PI*, 158). That's all. No shudders, echoes, glimpses of infinity. Ten words, two sentences. The only mystery, as far as he is concerned, is the oddity of Adela's behavior. He assumes that questions have answers, that "the true explanation [will be found] in a couple of days" (*PI*, 177). It is only when he sees the caves at a distance that he is dimly aware of their power. But the way that moment is described confirms the limitations of his vision: "As he gazed at the Marabar Hills they seemed to move graciously towards him like a queen, and their charm became the sky's. At the moment they vanished they were everywhere. . . . Lovely exquisite moment—but passing the Englishman with averted face and swift wings. He experienced nothing himself" (*PI*, 191). The passage occurs as Fielding is poised between two worlds. He has just had the angry confrontation in the club and given his resignation; moments later he will ride off "to his new allies" (*PI*, 191). He inhabits his life lightly, just as he is aware and not aware of the hills filling the sky. Thus it is significant that in the aftermath of the trial, when he finds himself doubly committed—to the victor Aziz and to the loser Adela—the memory of that moment returns, but the vision is then threatening and oppressive as he recalls "the evening after the catastrophe, when from the verandah of the club he saw the fists and fingers of the Marabar swell until they included the whole night sky" (*PI*, 250). They may stand for the catastrophe, but they are forever outside his range of experience.

As the narrative shifts to Adela, the word "fingers" provides a suggestive metaphoric link. Suffering from sunstroke, she is covered with cactus needles that have to be removed carefully lest they break and get drawn into her bloodstream. Miss Derek and Mrs. McBryde examine her with magnifying glasses, hour after hour picking the spines out of her flesh. "She lay passive beneath their fingers, which developed the shock that had begun in the cave" (*PI*, 193). Their fingers replace the Marabar fists and fingers, seeming to confound the cure with the cause of the sickness. Indeed, their ministrations exacerbate the injuries, sustaining the image of the cave as assailant, the body as violated object. The ordinary noun "sunstroke" is replaced by the phrase "she had been touched by the sun," as if the sun, too, were the assailant. It is an important detail, and it is, moreover, directly connected to the description of the caves in chapter 12: "If flesh of the sun's flesh is to be touched anywhere it is here" (*PI*, 123). It is as if her touching the cave wall let loose some primal power in the stone: "I remember scratching the wall with my finger nail, to start the usual echo, and then . . . there was this shadow, or sort of shadow, down the entrance tunnel, bottling me up" (*PI*, 193). Now as she lies inert, bottled up, her attempts to think things out are blocked by her body, and thought itself is reduced to an empty, repetitive echo. There is a curious synesthesia—that is, mixing of the senses, in this case the senses of touch and hearing—in the account of her depression, particularly concerning the echo: "The noise in the cave . . . was prolonged over the surface of her life" (*PI*, 194). The sound seems to be a substance, entering her body through the skin.

Both Fielding and Adela seek confirmation of their versions of events in someone else and both fail. Fielding's conversation with Godbole "culminated in a cow" (*PI*, 179)—that is, from Fielding's exasperated view, in a Brahman parable about good and evil, which he is unable and unwilling to follow. He maintains his belief in Aziz's innocence, but he refuses to consider the problem in terms larger than itself, especially in terms of Godbole's claim that we all have contributed to good and to evil. This, of course, is a position that the entire narrative probes as both a metaphysical and a political issue. Fielding's inability to recognize this, like his reaction to the caves, is further evidence of his limitations, of why he cannot be considered a touchstone character or an authorial surrogate.

The truth Adela seeks is less pragmatically verifiable; she is more willing than Fielding to accept the category of evil since she confronts it constantly in the echo, which, she imagines, only Mrs. Moore can "drive . . . back to its source" (*PI*, 194). She is right about one thing: only Mrs. Moore knows what she means by the echo. To Adela's statement, "I can't get rid of it," Mrs. Moore replies, "I don't suppose you ever will" (*PI*, 200). As Adela begins to confront the possibility that she might be wrong, that Aziz might be innocent, the echo dissipates, but Mrs. Moore refuses to help and the echo returns. Words, Mrs. Moore bitterly remarks, are useless: "Say, say, say . . . as if anything can be said" (*PI*, 200). As the narrative moves closer to the trial, she dismisses as futile all attempts to get at the truth through evidence, through words: "I will not help you to torture him for what he never did" (*PI*, 205). Her reasons provide an unsettling parody of Godbole's discourse on good and evil: "When shall I be free from your fuss? Was he in the cave and were you in the cave and on and on . . . and unto us a Son is born, unto us a Child is given . . . and am I good and is he bad and are we saved? . . . and ending everything the echo" (*PI*, 205; ellipses in text). From her perspective the British preoccupation with the trial is mechanical and soulless; she sees that Adela "has started the machinery; it will work to its end" (*PI*, 206). Nonetheless, although she withdraws from the narrative with that remark as her last word, the dispute will be settled through her agency in ways she cannot possibly imagine and in a fashion that both validates and challenges the courtroom as the site of saying, of clarification, of truth.

As the narrative builds toward the climactic trial, there is a buildup as well of community tension over the Mohurram celebrations (a Muslim holiday often involving Hindu/Muslim confrontations and, this year, anti-British rioting as well). The fear of the eruption of the irrational that the Mohurram drums evoke recalls the caves episode; so does the accelerating heat. Indeed, the degree to which the two scenes share a similar atmosphere is remarkable. The description of "the annual helter-skelter of April, when irritability and lust spread like a canker" (*PI*, 211) sets the scene for the trial; it could easily apply to the disastrous picnic as well. Although both episodes share a complex metaphoric structure, they are in one sense polar opposites. For the trial is the site of interpretation; its function is to make sense of events. It offers a reading of the text from within the text by reviewing all the narrative elements and attempting to make them yield a story.

The trial scene was almost as difficult to write as the caves scene, although in the trial scene the problems had more to do with the ordering of details and accuracy in depicting courtroom procedures. Forster sent a draft of the chapter to Masood, asking for comments and corrections: "I am having such trouble with this chapter that I have typed it in rough and send it to you for your comments. Please let me have them as soon as possible. Shuttleworth thinks that the case is too important to be tried in a small local court, but I hope you are right; anyhow it now must be so; I only want not to be glaringly wrong."[2] Masood saw no difficulty, but Shuttleworth was, in fact, correct, as reviews and letters frequently pointed out. Forster's defense of himself to one of his critics, however, makes clear what he had hoped to accomplish in the trial scene, especially in the depiction of the behavior of the British: "Even if my technical errors over the arrest and trial were corrected, even if the alleged social solecisms (though these of course are more disputable) were altered to your liking, you would still dislike the book as a whole because of its reading of English psychology. The reading according to my lights is true and I am not disposed to modify it" (Furbank, 2:127). Problems with some technical details aside, the trial scene is in fact the most realistic in the novel, chiefly because of the allusions to actual events: the Rowlatt Acts, the Amritsar Massacre, the Non-Cooperation movement, and the brief Hindu/Muslim entente.

The trial scene provides the last massed chorus of the English characters; it is the culminating episode in the novel read as social criticism and satire. The trial as judicial procedure directly reflects the political ferment of the early 1920s, but as social ritual it is located decades earlier. Here the implicit anachronism in the social setting serves Forster's purposes well, for what we see is the breakdown of an authority that had been presumed safe from challenge. "A new spirit seemed abroad, a rearrangement, which no one in the stern little band of whites could explain" (PI, 214). In the trial itself this rearrangement is made comically literal in the choreography of the chairs that had "preceded them into the Court, for it was important that they should look dignified" (PI, 217). They are first placed below the platform, then up on the platform, then moved down from the platform. At the outset the British seem to take charge of the trial, but by the close, with "the flimsy framework of the court broke[n] up" (PI, 231), they are swept up in the confusion and rage, their authority and dignity in at least temporary disarray.

Far more important, however, than the satiric scaling down of the Turtons and McBrydes, is the central confrontation of the trial when Adela takes the witness stand. Here the trial becomes Adela's test, first as she resists the tribal pressure to conform, to play the symbolic role assigned her by the group, literally to speak the rehearsed words, and second as she faces her own darkness and attempts to make memory and language converge. She is helped in this process by two figures: the silent punkah wallah, the man who rhythmically pulls the fan in the hot courtroom, and Mrs. Moore.

Although the description of the punkah wallah is very little changed from the manuscripts, his function in the scene is altered in a revealing fashion. The emphasis in both versions is on his physical beauty despite the lowliness of his caste and the blankness of his mind. (The most inexplicable and meaningless of David Lean's many changes of detail in the movie version is to make this figure into a little wizened old man.) On one level he functions realistically as he performs a necessary and commonplace task, but on another he is an entirely symbolic figure, presiding over the destinies of the characters. Like a naked god, he seems "apart from human destinies, a male fate, a winnower of souls" (*PI*, 217). Originally his figure carried a greater sexual charge than it does in the final version: "He twisted back her mind to that moment on the great notched rock where she thought 'do I love Ronny,' . . . he was a link in a series that stretched back into mental darkness and had never been properly explored by her" (*Mss.*, 376). Immediately after this she sees Aziz and realizes at once that "he hadn't done it . . . she had made a mistake." Possibly Forster felt the linkage here to be a little too pat—the naked god, the animal on the Marabar Road, the nicked rock, the unanswered question about love, and the consequent realization that Aziz is innocent. Revised, the moment of revelation still contains the psychological and the sexual, but it is not limited to them. Indeed, her first reaction to the punkah wallah in the printed text is to question how Western civilization claims the right to impose its beliefs and norms upon the rest of the world: "Her particular brand of opinions, and the suburban Jehovah who sanctified them—by what right did they claim so much importance in the world, and assume the title of civilization?" (*PI*, 218). The realization of Aziz's innocence is much more gradual and involves the intervention of another figure altogether, that of her friend Mrs. Moore returned to the text as "a Hindu goddess" (*PI*, 225).

As with the punkah wallah, the realistic and the symbolic interweave subtly here. With the mention of her name comes the dispute over the Rowlatt Acts, which would have allowed the testimony of the absent or the dead. The position of the magistrate is unequivocal: "As a witness, Mrs. Moore does not exist" (*PI*, 226). But as a magical force, she is outside of his power. "In vain the Magistrate threatened and expelled. Until the magic exhausted itself, he was powerless" (*PI*, 225). A courtroom with its ritual gestures, costumes, and specialized language is itself a place of magic, of heightened reality, as much as of logic. Adela had feared the court as "the place of question" (*PI*, 228), where the connection between the disaster in the cave and her engagement might have to be "examined in public" (*PI*, 227). But since the tumultuous invocation of Mrs. Moore's name as "Esmiss Esmoor," it becomes a place of vision, of magic, as well: "The fatal day recurred, in every detail, but now she was of it and not of it, at the same time, and this double relation gave it indescribable splendour" (*PI*, 227). It is the reverse of the double vision of Mrs. Moore, for whom "the horror of the universe and its smallness [were] both visible at the same time" (*PI*, 207).

This is as close as we ever get to discovering what happened in the caves. We see the scene again through Adela's eyes. What had been perfunctory sightseeing is, in recollection, "beautiful and significant." But at the very center of this vision is nothing; the emptiness that was the defining feature of the caves appears in the syntax of her three statements: "I am not—"; "I am not quite sure"; "I cannot be sure" (*PI*, 229). In an earlier version, this is even more explicit: "The echo started, the shadow crept down the tunnel, and something in the center of her soul said 'No!' " (*Mss.*, 399). The shadow will not materialize: "She failed to locate him" (*PI*, 229).

The courtroom and all the procedures of British justice have barely been able to contain the contending forces. Was it a parody of a judicial proceeding? The attitude of the superintendent of police—"everyone knows the man's guilty, and I am obliged to say so in public before he goes to the Andamans" (*PI*, 218)—suggests as much. Or can one see it as a nearly heroic attempt to make a suspect institution work just sufficiently to allow a minimum of justice? From one point of view, the trial is a failure; it reveals nothing of what happened. However, from Aziz's point of view, the trial is a success, albeit a mysterious one, with Mrs. Moore somehow giving her testimony on his behalf.

The trial ends but the questions remain. What happened both in the cave and in the courtroom? How does one even formulate such questions? What is just compensation? Is any compensation possible? What remains of friendships and alliances in a world that has been permanently altered? These questions are not left to be inferred. They are a direct part of what the characters talk about, for talk is pretty much all that happens for the next several chapters as the world of mosque and cave, bridge party and tea party, seeing India and Indians, slowly unravels. In the scenes between Fielding and Aziz and the parallel ones between Fielding and Adela, this sorry aftermath is played out. At the center of each is a sense of diminishment, of lost possibilities, that disorienting sense that Fielding has after the trial that "we exist not in ourselves, but in terms of each other's minds" (*PI*, 250). Mrs. Moore, entirely absent as a character, is a ghostly presence in these scenes. She is part of the theme of the uncanny that requires that we reconsider the narrative, not as a detective story with a central mystery to disclose but as a ghost story, one which in fact began at the start of the novel, in the mosque, when "one of the pillars . . . seemed to quiver . . . belief in ghosts ran in [Aziz's] blood . . . another pillar moved, a third, and then an Englishwoman stepped out into the moonlight" (*PI*, 20).

10

Endings

To the interviewer's question about the function of the long description of the Hindu festival in the third section, Forster replied, "It was architecturally necessary. I needed a lump, or a Hindu temple if you like—a mountain standing up. It is well placed; and it gathers up some strings. But there ought to be more after it. The lump sticks out a little too much" (*Paris Review*, 10). The point about architecture is important. It suggests how carefully structured the novel is, how precisely articulated are its parts. But Forster is also referring here to the architecture of the Hindu temple itself, and he is doing so in the language he had used some years before the interview to describe an exhibit of photographs from India. Speaking on a broadcast in 1940 on the Eastern Service of the BBC, he said he had learned in India "that the Hindu temple symbolizes the world mountain, on whose sides gods, man and animals are sculptured in all their complexity. . . . The inside is a very different story. The dark of the Hindu temple is a promenade, leading to a dark central cell, the sanctuary, where the individual makes contact with the divine principle. . . . [I]t was with relief and joy that I saw these great temples where the individual is at the last resort alone with his god, buried in the depths of the world mountain" (*Hill*, 238–39). Although this is something he claims to have learned about Hinduism after the writing of *A Passage to India*, his response of joy and relief suggests a confirmation of his own intuition about the central crisis of his novel. His language in this broadcast interestingly anticipates his comments on the Marabar Caves in the *Paris Review* interview: all his novels, he said in the interview, contained "a solid mass ahead, a mountain round or over or through which the story must somehow go. . . . [T]he Malabar [*sic*] caves represented an area in which concentration can take place, a cavity" (*Paris Review*, 9).

MRS. MOORE

The language Forster used to describe both the caves and the temple has an interesting application to Mrs. Moore as well. Since she occupies so important a position in the design if not in the plot of the novel, it is useful to identify the ways in which she participates in the novel's close, particularly her return to the text transformed through the trial into the Hindu deity "Esmiss Esmoor." Like the caves, she can be described as a figure "in which concentration can take place." Although she does very little as a character, it is through her that all the critical relationships of the novel are established and interpreted, that is, "concentrated." Like the caves, she carries a symbolic function far in excess of her narrative function, and she is, too, a figure of the caves, that is, a figure of negation and emptiness. Not only did the echo that she heard there "undermine her hold on life" (*PI*, 149), but it also produced the twilight state of double vision where infinity, eternity, even the abyss, what the narrator calls the "large things," seemed reduced and petty. Unfortunately for her, and indeed for all the characters in the novel, the god she encountered in the depth of the world mountain was "something snub nosed, incapable of generosity—the undying worm itself" (*PI*, 208).

Thus any attempt to say what *A Passage to India* is "about" involves saying what Mrs. Moore is about, but that—as Santha Rama Rau, who adapted the novel for the stage, pointed out—is nearly impossible: "Although she is a pivotal character and expresses much of what the novel and the play are trying to say, she remained obstinately allusive, illusive and inarticulate. An inexplicable, but absolutely convincing, symbol in the book, but maddening when one has to transfer her to the stage." Rama Rau recalled asking Forster, "She's got to speak, but every time I try to give her words for her thoughts, she comes out sounding false . . .

how will the audience *know* what goes on in her head?" (Natwar-Singh, 52). *Allusive, illusive, inarticulate, inexplicable*—these words describing her presence in the text point to the technical difficulty of making her speak on a stage. They are even more to the point when after her death she flits in and out of the lives of the other characters as a disembodied, even ghostly, presence.

Her importance is, nonetheless, quite disproportionate to her minimal role in the plot. "What did this eternal goodness of Mrs. Moore amount to?" Aziz wonders. "To nothing, if brought to the test of thought. She had not borne witness in his favor, nor visited him in the prison, yet she had stolen to the depths of his heart, and he always adored her" (*PI*, 312). Thus it is in her afterlife in the consciousness of the novel's characters that she has the greatest effect. In this regard, her role is very similar to that of Mrs. Wilcox in *Howards End.* Replying to an interviewer's question about Mrs. Wilcox, Forster remarked, "I was interested in the imaginative effect of someone alive, but in a different way from other characters—living in other lives" (*Paris Review*, 11). He could just as well have been describing Mrs. Moore.

From the moment of her death she assumes a new status in the novel. Indeed, even before her death is known to the other characters she has a transfiguring function when she is invoked as a Hindu deity at the trial. And as her death is discussed by the other characters it becomes the occasion for raising the central issues of the novel. In the final section she directly "live[s] in other lives," first in the vision Godbole has of her and then through her son Ralph who draws from Aziz the same words he had spoken to her in the mosque, as if the cycle were beginning again.

Her death is first reported by Fielding. He has just learned of it from her son and tells Hamidullah. There is regret but no great emotion; their immediate concern is to keep the news from Aziz so as not to spoil his victory celebration. But the narrator uses the occasion of Mrs. Moore's death to pose the frequently recurring questions: how comprehensive is human sympathy? how inclusive is the human community? "If for a moment the sense of communion in sorrow came to them, it passed. How indeed is it possible for one human being to be sorry for all the sadness that meets him on the face of the earth, for the pain that is endured not only by men, but by animals and plants, and perhaps by the stones?" (*PI*,

247). It is a rhetorical question in this context. The implicit answer from the point of view of Fielding and Hamidullah is "impossible," but that is an admission of defeat: "The soul is tired in a moment, and in fear of losing the little she does understand, she retreats to the permanent lines which habit or chance have dictated, and suffers there" (*PI*, 247–48). Yet the very phrasing of the question suggests a vision of continuity and inclusiveness very much in the spirit of an observation Forster had made a few years earlier in *Alexandria: A History and a Guide*: "We're all part of God, even the stones."[1] The exchange between Fielding and Hamidullah also refers back to the missionaries' difficulty with this notion in the early passage on the meaning of invitation. They drew a line—"we must exclude someone from our gathering, or we shall be left with nothing" (*PI*, 38)—but the narrative that follows challenges even that possibly necessary complacency.

The issue of inclusion/exclusion also occurs in the final section of the novel, most notably in Godbole's dance before the altar, and it is once again through the uncanny intervention of Mrs. Moore. Suddenly Godbole "remembered an old woman he had met in Chandrapore days . . . [H]e did not select her, she happened to occur amid the throng of soliciting images . . . [H]e remembered a wasp seen he forgot where, perhaps on a stone. He loved the wasp equally, he impelled it likewise, he was imitating God. And the stone where the wasp clung—could he . . . [ellipses in text], no, he could not, he had been wrong to attempt the stone." And yet his vision of infinite love in the form of Shri Krishna that follows does attempt to encompass the stone, for in it "all sorrow was annihilated not only for Indians, but for foreigners, birds, caves, railways, and the stars" (*PI*, 286–88). For Godbole the connection is simple, "one old Englishwoman and one little, little wasp . . . It does not seem much, still it is more than I am myself" (*PI*, 291). Somewhat fancifully, one might say that the wasp that makes the connection is the wasp that Mrs. Moore did not kill when she found it on the coat peg the evening of her first Indian day. "Pretty dear," she had said instead (*PI*, 35), and by that intuitive act of sympathy she set herself apart from the Anglo-Indian world and initiated the process of her transfiguration into a Hindu goddess. (When asked if "the wasps [had] any esoteric meaning," Forster replied, "Only in the sense that there is something esoteric in India about all animals. I was just putting it in; and afterwards I saw it was something that might return non-logically in the story later" [*Paris Review*, 15]. That is, the wasp does not have a direct symbolic translation, but belongs to a subtextual pattern of correspondences that may also be related to the Jain belief discussed previously that all of nature is alive and connected.)

Thus on the symbolic level, Mrs. Moore may function as a figure of reconciliation, as she, like Mrs. Wilcox in *Howards End*, lives in other lives; on the merely human level, however, she is considerably less satisfactory. The critic Reuben Brower states the problem in a useful fashion: "We cannot at the end of the novel regard Mrs. Moore as in tune with the infinite and conveniently forget the mocking denial of her echo."[2] However, it is this very doubleness that makes her even more convincing as a Hindu goddess, like Kali containing powers that are both destructive and nurturing. As a split figure she epitomizes the entire text, which also can be read for its aesthetic satisfactions, for its reconciling of patterns and symbols, those wasps and stones, trees and snakes, fists and fingers. But the human drama in all its messy particularity that is played out against this intricate backdrop resists, even denies, such neat patterning. In the final section, one may observe this dual tendency very clearly.

GODBOLE AND THE BIRTH OF KRISHNA

"Temple" is part of two different structural patterns, what one might describe, using Forster's other novels as reference points, as the *Howards End* and *The Longest Journey* structures. As in *Howards End*, where Hertfordshire and London are antithetic places, but where Hertfordshire finally absorbs the alien, urban world, the "Temple" section completes what "Mosque" began; it provides antithesis and the possibility of fulfillment. The overarching triadic structure of the novel, however, is directly reminiscent of the three-part structure of *The Longest Journey*'s Cambridge, Sawston, and Wiltshire. One can find several parallels between Sawston and the "Caves" section, not least among them the relationship of the concluding sections to the central darkness. For "Temple" not only offers a tentative solution to the human dilemmas raised in "Caves" but also transforms, at least temporarily, the frightening darkness of the empty cavity of the Kawa Dol into a space of celebration.

The celebration is the Gokul Ashtami, the eight-day festival centering on the birth of Krishna. It celebrates birth, but it is also the occasion of death. It reconciles friends but it also provides the occasion for their final separation. Against this backdrop the narrator attempts to find a synthesis at once aesthetic, ethical, and political. It is, no doubt, an impossible task, made the more difficult by the very varying responses of the reader to the description of the festival and in particular to the character of Godbole.

Critics tend to divide over Godbole; to some he is a fool, a clown; to others, the ethical center of the text. That the narrator has some fun at his expense is obvious. There is a note of comedy in the description of the pince-nez caught in the jasmine garland (*PI*, 284) in the opening chapter of "Temple," or, earlier, in his first appearance at Fielding's tea party: "He wore a turban that looked like pale purple macaroni, coat, waistcoat, dhoti, socks with clocks. . . . The ladies were interested in him, and hoped that he would supplement Dr. Aziz by saying something about religion. But he only ate—ate, and ate, smiling, never letting his eyes catch sight of his hand" (*PI*, 72–73). His conversation may "culminate in a cow," he may seem exasperatingly evasive when asked a direct question, but all this is to say that he stands outside the experience and the codes for that experience of the English characters. For the most part the narrator keeps him at a distance, never, except in the opening chapter of the final section, speaking from his position. Indeed, Godbole barely participates in the plot at all except by inadvertence. Had he not "miscalculated the length of a prayer" (*PI*, 131), he and Fielding would not have missed the train and none of the events would have unfolded as they did. Here again narrative structure and theme are complexly intertwined, for as Godbole explains to Fielding: "Nothing can be performed in isolation. All perform a good action, when one is performed, and when an evil action is performed, all perform it" (*PI*, 177). Fielding, however, remains an uncomprehending listener, convinced that cause and effect describe a single, linear, discrete relationship that can unambiguously be brought to light. As we have seen, the response that Fielding finds so exasperating, when what he wanted was a straightforward declaration of belief in Aziz's innocence, is not very different from Adela's at the trial: "I am not quite sure" (*PI*, 229). And it is little different finally from that of the narrator, who refuses to collapse his narrative into a simple declarative statement, or from that of the author, who willed his mind to remain a blur. I would suggest that Godbole cannot be the ethical center of the text, if for no other reason than that the novel is constructed around an empty center. However, he can offer a legitimate response in ethical terms to the dilemmas posed there. It may be a position that is essentially out of reach of the other characters and one that the narrator never entirely assents to, but it holds out a prophetic possibility that colors and deepens the political and social realism of the novel's close.

The tone of the description of the festival is similarly hard to assess. The narrator seems to switch from approval to skepticism, from admiration to amusement, from participation to the keeping of a considerable distance, as he evokes the festivities with something of a Western dismay at the "muddle (as we call it), a frustration of reason and form" (*PI*, 285). When he allows Godbole to focus the scene, however, it becomes larger than the jumble (from a Western point of view) of its details. Like David dancing before the ark (2 Sam. 6), Godbole clashes his cymbals, "his little legs twinkling, his companions dancing with him and each other" (*PI*, 286). In that ecstasy everything for the moment coheres—the birth of the lord, Mrs. Moore, the wasp—but the moment is fleeting and finally inexpressible. "How can it be expressed in anything but itself?" (*PI*, 288).

That question perhaps explains why Hinduism is not finally offered as a solution, either in thematic, psychological, or political terms. The narrator positions himself between those Westerners who regard the sign on the palace wall, "God si love," as yet one more example of the careless East (the collar stud problem) and those who read in "the unfortunate slip of the draughtsman" (*PI*, 285) different but equally valid utterances of religious affirmation—God yes love; God if love; God is love; God see(s) love; and, what is even more foreign to the orderly and decorous Western imagination, that God might make a joke about love. " 'God si love!' There is fun in heaven, God can play jokes upon Himself, draw chairs away from beneath His own posteriors, set His own turbans on fire. . . . By sacrificing good taste, this worship achieved what Christianity has shirked: the inclusion of merriment. All spirit as well as all matter must participate in salvation, and if practical jokes are banned, the circle is incomplete" (*PI*, 289). This line provides one more perspective on the exclusion/inclusion problem but in such a way as to leave the Western observer—or, more particularly, the non-Hindu observer—outside that happy circle. The narrator's sympathies are clearly with those who find merriment in religion. He uses the draughtsman's slip to suggest the limitations of the Western tendency to correct, to get it right, the distinction made earlier (indeed immediately following the collar stud scene) between verbal truth and truth of mood (*PI*, 72). However, the scene as a whole remains just that—a scene, a staged event before which all the characters (except of course Godbole) are spectators. It is finally as an untranslatable event, something that can be expressed only as itself, that the Gokul Ashtami festivities provide the setting for the final set of meetings and partings that conclude the novel.

ALTERED RELATIONSHIPS

Among the characters there are those who are closer to the Hindu solution than others—fittingly the children of the Hindu goddess, Esmiss Esmoor. But the central character of the final section, Aziz, is not; in many ways he is as far from understanding Hinduism as is Fielding. Except for the opening chapter, which is for the most part focalized through Godbole, the narrator aligns his point of view with Aziz throughout this section. It is, of course, an outsider's point of view. A Muslim doctor in a Hindu Native State, Aziz discovers that "the cleavage [in Mau] was between Brahman and non-Brahman; Moslems and English were quite out of the running, and sometimes not mentioned for days" (*PI*, 292). His move to Mau is in a sense paradoxical, for by choosing to live in a remote Native State instead of actively engaging in political activity, he would seem to stand apart from the struggle for independence. But the terms of his apparent disengagement have a direct symbolic and political value. For it is at Mau that he can feel himself "an Indian at last" (*PI*, 293), not somebody's servant, but at home in his own country, having completed one kind of passage to India.

Although Aziz reaches this point emotionally, he remains aware of the difficulties it entails, aware of the vast differences of belief and custom among his countrymen. "There is no such person in existence as the general Indian," Aziz had said earlier (*PI*, 266), and the novel has both challenged and confirmed that utterance. He is still the Muslim poet of bulbuls and roses, only too conscious of the fact that "the fissures in the Indian soil are infinite" (*PI*, 292). Indeed the only one of his poems that had appealed to Godbole "was one that had gone straight to internationality" (*PI*, 293), bypassing altogether the difficult problems of nationality. Internationalism, however valuable in itself, may well be a necessity when there are so many competing nationalisms on one soil. Yet by the close of the novel Aziz has embraced the nationalist position. The narrator may stand apart from such a conclusion, neither endorsing nor resisting it. But Aziz, he makes quite clear, does not have the luxury of such detachment. If his primary motive in going to Mau was to escape the English, he discovers that even there he has still not entirely eluded the watchful eye of the Raj: "The Criminal Investigation Department kept an eye on Aziz ever since the trial—they had nothing actionable against him, but Indians who have been unfortunate must be watched, and to the end of his life he remained under observation, thanks to Miss Quested's mistake" (*PI*, 294).

It is important to hear the irony of that last line, for however many spiritual trials Adela may have undergone, she is now safe at home, no doubt even improved by her experience, in thoughtful, artistic Hampstead. Not so Aziz whose world has been turned upside down, who remains a suspect person to the police and to the rest of the civil servants who "knew" his guilt whatever Adela did or did not say at the trial. In Mau he is away from the particulars of that event, but he has been altered permanently so that between him and the English—even Fielding, even the son and daughter of Mrs. Moore—there is a barrier that cannot be crossed until political relations are fundamentally changed.

One measure of the altered relationships is the handling of the Fielding character. The shift is relatively slight; he is still the loyal, affectionate friend, but having become the Anglo-Indian he is cut off from his own past. "He had thrown in his lot with Anglo India . . . and already felt surprise at his own past heroism. Would he to-day defy all his own people for the sake of a stray Indian?" (*PI*, 319). The phrase, "stray Indian," might surprise us more had we not already seen the letter from Heaslop to Fielding that Aziz reads when he comes to the guest house to see to Ralph Moore's bee sting: "I'm relieved you feel able to come into line with the Oppressors of India. . . . You are lucky to be out of British India at the present moment. Incident after incident, all due to propaganda, but we can't lay our hands on the connecting thread. The longer one lives here, the more certain one gets that everything hangs together. My personal opinion is, it's the Jews" (*PI*, 307–8). By putting this at the remove of Ronny's letter, neither the narrator nor the other characters have to account for or even allude to the change. We assume that Fielding will keep his distance from the colonial paranoia that the letter reveals and will not respond as Ronny intended to the ironic disdain of "Oppressors." Fielding will no doubt have his reservations, but they will be privately held. Not "defy[ing] his own people" means doing his imperial duty, and with that duty comes a whole set of reflexes and catchwords whatever his private demurrals. Forster uses the letter to make clear what sort of baggage Fielding must carry around with him now that he is no longer traveling light. The allusion to an international Jewish conspiracy is shorthand for a wide range of popular beliefs that were also staples of contemporary Anglo-Indian fiction. Flora Annie Steel's *The Law of the Threshold*, for example, contains this passage: "Mr. Markovitch, a Russian Jew, who in banking circles was known as Mr. Markham . . . repeated the famous Bolshevist toast—'To the destruction of Law and Order and the unchaining of Evil Passions' " (Steel, 36–37). Later in the novel, one of the characters says, "I'm going to have a stab at finding out what is at the bottom of everything. I believe it's the Bolsheviks" (Steel, 152). In the world Ronny moves in there is nothing exceptional about his speech or his beliefs; now that world is Fielding's, too. From its vantage, Aziz is only a stray Indian, "a memento, a trophy" (*PI*, 319) from an irrecoverable past.

The scene in the guest house between Aziz and Ralph Moore, however, does at least momentarily recover the past. Aziz responds to the son as he had to the mother, who is herself a palpable presence in the twilight room. The meeting, the recognition of friendship, the gestures of hospitality—all the motifs that constitute the novel we have read are replayed within this last encounter as the

Gokul Ashtami celebrations reach their climax. Birth and death are also oddly intertwined, for the Rajah's death occurs in the midst of the festivities. It is kept secret until after the festival, "to prevent unhappiness," just as the death of Mrs. Moore was kept from Aziz lest it spoil the victory celebration that followed the trial. During this scene it is Ralph, with his intuitive sympathy for Hinduism, who directs Aziz's gaze to the one spot on the lake where the statue of the Rajah's father is visible; it is Ralph who is more guide than guest and whom Aziz obeys, for "he knew in his heart that this was Mrs. Moore's son, and indeed until his heart was involved he knew nothing" (*PI*, 313). And as the chant "Radhakrishna, Radhakrishna" is repeated, Aziz "heard, almost certainly, the syllables of salvation that had sounded during his trial at Chandrapore" (*PI*, 314)—the name of Mrs. Moore, audible to his ears alone.

There are in a sense two final scenes—the collision on the lake where all the characters come together and move apart in a pantomime scene of reconciliation and parting, and the last ride together of Aziz and Fielding. They are framed by variations on the same sentence, so that any interpretation of the last enigmatic sentence of the novel must begin a few pages earlier when the boat carrying Aziz and Ralph drifts into the final ceremonies just before it collides with the boat carrying Fielding and his wife, Stella Moore, and just at the moment when the God is thrown into the waters: "Thus was He thrown year after year, and others were thrown— little images of Ganpati, baskets of ten-day corn, tiny tazias after Mohurram—scapegoats, husks, emblems of passage; *a passage not easy, not now, not here, not to be apprehended except when it is unattainable: the God to be thrown was an emblem of that*" (*PI*, 314–15; my italics). The presiding figure of this scene, the servitor who carries into the lake the replica of the village of Gokul, the birthplace of Krishna, is a reprise of the punkah wallah, the naked godlike figure who rhythmically moved the fan in the courtroom. There he was described as a winnower of souls; here he has much the same description and function: "He was naked, broad-shouldered, thin-waisted—the Indian body again triumphant—and it was his hereditary office to close the gates of salvation" (*PI*, 315).

But who is inside those gates, and who is outside? Where is it better to be? How have these ceremonies touched the three English visitors and their Muslim friend? Since Forster uses symbolism in a suggestive rather than in an allegorical fashion (meanings are allowed to proliferate; they are not translatable or equatable), there are no clear-cut answers to such questions. The rain, the wind, the water carry their mythic potential, especially through the vocabulary they share with texts like *The Waste Land*, but they are not invested with transcendental meaning. Two kinds of action, the sacred and the profane, proceed simultaneously, but they are connected only loosely. The ceremonies may illuminate or deepen the meeting between Aziz and Fielding, between Aziz and the children of his beloved Mrs. Moore, but they do not explain or conclude it. Rather the ceremonies awake in each participant "an emotion that he would not have had otherwise" (*PI*, 290), although it is not identifiable, either for the celebrants or for the friends: "Looking back at the great blur of the last twenty-four hours, no man could say where was the emotional center of it, any more than he could locate the heart of a cloud" (*PI*, 316). Pieces of the past and present float confusedly on the waters after the boats capsize, a fitting image for the failure of the reconciliation.

Nothing surprising occurs in the final scene. That it is the last time Fielding and Aziz will meet is clear from the first sentence. The friends recapture something of their intimacy but there is no space either in the fiction or in the world they inhabit where they can meet. Goodwill is not enough; it certainly cannot transform political institutions. One thinks back to Mrs. Moore's belief that "one touch of regret" might transform the British Empire, and one realizes how useless whole armfuls of regret would be. Both Fielding and Aziz know this, but the scene takes its momentum from Fielding's attempt to act as if past relationships could be reestablished, as if his marriage were not a double betrayal, both of that intimacy and of his independence from the Raj. Aziz, however, is changed entirely. With remarkable prescience, considering the Congress party's refusal to join the British at the start of the Second World War, he calls on the British to clear out of India: "Clear out, clear out, I say. Why are we put to so much suffering? We used to blame you, now we blame ourselves, we grow wiser. Until England is in difficulties we keep silent, but in the next European war—aha, aha! Then is our time" (*PI*, 321). Forster carries the political theme to the end, making it very clear that political change must precede transformed social relations. The process is not reversible; there can be no friendship where there is inequality. " '[I]f it's fifty or five hundred years we shall get rid of you . . . and then . . . and then,' he concluded half kissing him, 'you and I shall be friends' " (*PI*, 322). But there is more a sense of inevitability than optimism in the narrator's voice when he comments on the earlier speech of Aziz: "The scenery, though it smiled, fell like a gravestone on any human hope" (*PI*, 321).

THE LAST SENTENCE

> But the horses didn't want it—they swerved apart; the earth didn't want it, sending up rocks through which the riders must pass single file; the temples, the tank, the jail, the palace, the birds, the carrion, the Guest House, that came into view as they issued from the gap and saw Mau beneath: they didn't want it, they said in their hundred voices, "No, not yet," and the sky said, "No, not there." (*PI*, 322)

The tone is elegiac, even wistful, but the point is uncompromising. The very soil prevents connection. The riders go in single file; it is as if the Marabar had followed them to Mau, "sending up rocks" through the soil, enforcing the separation. The nouns, too, are lined up in the sentence in a catalog syntax. But this linear structure is placed in a metrical pattern of pairing that begins in the preceding passage, "and then . . . and then," and continues through the parallels and pairings of "the horses didn't / the earth didn't / they didn't" to the final "no not yet" and "no not there." Syntactically there is both separation and union, exclusion and inclusion. Does the "and then" allow a qualified hope for the "not yet"? Possibly, especially if one recalls the earlier version of this phrase—"a passage, not easy, not now, not here"—but the persistently negative syntax in both cases does not give much support to that frail hope.

At the end there is both aesthetic closure and thematic openness. The loose threads that Forster referred to in the *Paris Review* interview are gathered up, verbal patterns are completed, the characters are rearranged beneath the same overarching sky that opened the text and that is here given the last word. Is this an escape, as some critics would have it, into the containment of art?

Do we have in the ending the typically modernist gesture of standing outside the press of history, accomplished through the device of "absolute irony," what Alan Wilde describes as equal and opposed possibilities held in total poise?[3] I think not. The last sentence records not so much poise between but involvement in opposed positions or values, what one might loosely call the private and the public spheres. The narrator clearly would like a world where personal relations, what he had earlier called human hope, could triumph, but it is he who lowers the gravestone on such desire. Fielding, possibly, remains the elegist for this lost hope, but he has become a much-diminished character by this point. Whatever he may say, he has, in his brother-in-law's words, "come into line." Aziz, however, has been energized by the narrative. He does not function here as a means for another's spiritual crisis, as he had in the central section, but stands ready to make his own passage through history, although he no more than the narrator knows where that path will lead.

11

Epilogue:
Ghosts and Memory

An epilogue is a good place for ghosts, for the trace of the unspoken in the text. How does bringing this textual space to light alter any of the readings we have established? What does it mean to read *A Passage to India* as a ghost story?

To pose the question "What happened in the caves?" is to read the novel as a mystery story, which is in fact how one reads most novels. We want to solve a problem, to make the pieces of information that we have accumulated as readers cohere into a pattern of cause and effect. But to pose and withdraw such a question, to realize that it cannot be answered and that at the center of the text is a secret that cannot be disclosed, is to read *A Passage to India* as a ghost story. This is not an arbitrary reading strategy. Ghosts are part of the vocabulary of the novel. They link the psychological, metaphysical, political, and personal levels of the text. They enter the conversation of the characters and the speculation of the narrator, and they inhabit the memory of the writer, for *A Passage to India* contains Forster's ghosts, too. Thus by way of epilogue we will consider the supernatural in Forster's text and assess the cumulative effect of his ghosts in an effort to understand the relationship between the ghost story and the novel of friendship and empire.

The narrator never entirely commits himself to one narrative mode or the other, either to the mystery story or to the ghost story. He seems to push the narrative toward revelation but then he withdraws. This maneuver is partly the result of constructing the narrative around an empty center that contains nothing but that is so placed as constantly to solicit attempts at penetration and interpretation. It is also a function of the narrator's position within the text, which is located between the physical and the metaphysical, between his characters' consciousness and his own voice. There is a teasing quality to the narrative, what one student has called Forster's coy metaphysics. In part this quality derives from the narrator's never quite saying what he means, taking as his own stance what Forster described in a 1914 review as the essential quality of Hinduism, that "it is athirst for the inconceivable. Whatever can be stated must be temporary."[1] The narrator's voice tends to trail off into a silence that is meant to resonate beyond itself. This teasing quality also derives from the persistent casting of the physical in metaphysical terms. The "spurious unity," for example, that occurs when Adela and Ronny are jolted together moments before the accident in the Nawab Bahadur's car is given a cosmic backdrop in "the night that encircled them [that], absolute as it seemed, was itself only a spurious unity, being modified by the gleams of day that leaked up round the edges of the earth, and by the stars" (*PI*, 88).

This image also provides a useful way to identify the doubleness of the novel as a whole, its moving between the ratiocinative and supernatural modes, its presentation of a mystery story as a ghost story. For shadowing the primary narrative there seems to be another text, invisible and inaudible to nearly all the characters save Mrs. Moore and Ralph (and Stella, too, except that she is essentially an extra in the cast, important for marking the limits of Fielding's character but given no role of her own). This "other" novel, at once subtext and containing text, is situated just at the verge of his characters' consciousness. The narrator allows Fielding the reflection, for example, that "everything echoes now; there's no stopping the echo. The original sound may be harmless, but the echo is always evil," and then comments, "this reflection about the echo lay at the verge of Fielding's mind. He could never develop it. It belonged to the universe that he had missed or rejected" (*PI*, 276). What looks like direct quotation is really the narrator thinking through his character, nudging his narrative toward larger, but not quite statable, meaning. On the other side of the reflection that Fielding does not quite make lies a ghostly narrative, "the universe

he missed or rejected," of which he has only the dimmest awareness. The echo is the trace of that other text.

Since Fielding is a character who functions entirely within the
boundary of the conscious text, he could not possibly be the privileged center of consciousness of the novel; indeed, he is not even
particularly well equipped to read it. He neither hears the echo nor
possesses the "double vision" of Mrs. Moore. He sees but does not
see the Marabar at the last moment of light, when it seems to move
toward him as he watches from the club veranda on the night of the
catastrophe: "lovely exquisite moment—but passing the Englishman with averted face and on swift wings. He experienced nothing
himself" (*PI*, 191). There is a similar moment in the last of the conversations between Fielding and Adela after the trial. It occurs
when the narrator uses the remarkable image of dwarfs shaking
hands to establish the limitations and the paucity of their emotions
as well as their distance from even these diminished feelings. As
they say good-bye, "wistfulness descended on them . . . the shadow
of the shadow of a dream fell over their clear-cut interests, and
objects never seen again seemed messages from another world" (*PI*,
264–65). It is the narrator who registers the passing of this shadow,
the message from another world; Fielding and Adela merely shake
hands and part. The reader is given access to this realm through
the narrator's intervention in passages such as those just cited and
also in the frequent allusions to darkness, dreams, shadows, death,
and ghosts. The ghost story is entirely a trace text; it occurs in the
spaces of the primary text, in dreams, memories, old photographs,
and flashes of intuition that do not quite resolve, that the characters can never quite recall.

What I have been calling the shadow text is part of the narrative universe of the novel; it dwarfs the characters but it also gives
context to their actions, words, and gestures. But the ghostly works
on another less predictable and controllable level where it marks
the uncanny, the sudden coming to light of that which "ought to
have remained hidden and secret," as Freud described it in his
essay, "The Uncanny."[2] The "sudden coming to light" in Forster's
text, however, does not so much involve the sense of sight as the
senses of sound and touch: the "vile naked thing" that struck Mrs.
Moore's face, the scratch on the smooth skin of the cave wall, and
the sound of the echo, "boum," the sign of the unspeakable. The

uncanny is part of the narrative design, but it also marks that which the writer cannot entirely control. The eruption of the uncanny is both something that the writer stages—that is, that he makes happen to his characters—and something that happens to him as well.

The caves are, of course, the most obvious site of disruption/eruption; what happens there echoes through all the textual levels. That scene, moreover, is explicitly linked within the narrative structure to an earlier scene of ghostly menace, the accident on the Marabar Road. It may be useful to set out the scenes for comparison. As Adela and Aziz climb the hot hillside toward the fatal caves, "something repressed recurs," in Freud's words, but this manifestation of the "uncanny is in reality nothing new or alien, but something which is familiar and old-established in the mind" (Freud, 634).

> As she toiled over a rock that resembled an inverted saucer, she thought, "what about love?" The rock was nicked by a double row of footholds, and somehow the question was suggested by them. Where had she seen footholds before? Oh yes, they were the pattern traced in the dust by the wheels of the Nawab Bahadur's car. She and Ronny—no, they did not love each other. . . . There was esteem and animal contact at dusk, but the emotion that links them was absent. (*PI*, 151–52)

The nicked footholds call up the earlier scene:

> [T]he animal had probably come up out of the mullah. Steady and smooth ran the marks of the car, ribbons neatly nicked with lozenges, then all went mad. . . . Adela in her excitement knelt and swept her skirts about, until it was she if anyone who appeared to have attacked the car. (*PI*, 89)

When Ronny and Adela, who have become engaged to be married as a result of "animal contact at dusk," describe the accident to Mrs. Moore as she plays her game of solitaire, her response is "A ghost!" (*PI*, 97). The words seem to escape her unawares, for shortly after, when Adela questions her, she seems to have forgotten. Oddly though, her intuition is confirmed. In a parallel scene we learn from the Nawab Bahadur that indeed a ghost had been there, the ghost of the man he had run over on that road nine years earlier, who had "continued to wait in an unspeakable form, close to the scene of his death" (*PI*, 99).

The incident has both a supernatural and a psychological resonance. On one level it keeps up the connection between Mrs. Moore and the Indian spirit, although even for Mrs. Moore the connection is largely subconscious: "Didn't you say, 'Oh, a ghost,' in passing?" Adela asks. "I couldn't have been thinking of what I was saying," Mrs. Moore replies (*PI*, 103). But even if there is a residual skepticism about ghosts, there is a sense in which some unnamed power is at work. Aziz, for example, remains aloof when he hears the Nawab's frightened talk, for he recalls that it was by despising ghosts, by defying superstition, that he was able to call out to Mrs. Moore in the moonlit mosque and hence initiate the events that make up the novel. Given subsequent events, however, that aloofness is itself challenged, for Aziz is clearly out of his depth in the Marabar, unaware of its dangers, deaf to the power of its echo.

Part animal, part ghost, part the emblem of a sexual force felt as something external to and impinging on the self, the hairy animal (goat? buffalo? hyena?) that "rushed up out of the dark and hit" the car is at the center of a complex set of associations. The characters are no more able to name it than the reader. On one level, it becomes, like the green bird, an aspect of an India forever beyond the comprehension and control of the English: "The bird in question dived into the dome of the tree. . . . they would have liked to identify it. . . . but nothing in India is identifiable" (*PI*, 85–86). The animal on the Marabar Road can thus be read as an emblem of the unknown felt as threatening, as something violent and violating. However, Adela had called it "my hyena," as if it were something within her (remember the confusion made by her skirts in the dust). As it recurs to her memory it seems to enter the cave with her, emblem and instrument of an undefinable sexual threat that seems to inhere in the very landscape.

One must pursue such an approach carefully and nonreductively to avoid an argument where the animal = repressed desire = hallucination. Such a reading is not so much wrong as inadequate, certainly disproportionate to the elaborate metaphysical machinery wheeled into place to probe the experience in the cave. For whatever happened there, it is more than one person's neuroses or unhappiness, and, shifting the discussion from the psychological to the political, it signifies more than the paradox of British rule. Even a reading that would merge these approaches does not seem sufficiently explanatory. O. Mannoni's analysis of the psychosexual dynamics of colonialism, for example, can illuminate the passage, but it cannot account entirely for what happens in Forster's text. Using the French in Madagascar as his example, Mannoni described a process of sexual displacement in terms of what he called, referring to Shakespeare's *The Tempest*, a Prospero/Caliban paradigm: "The observer is repelled by the thoughts he encounters in his own mind, and it seems to him that they are the thoughts of the people he is observing."[3] Such an account may explain the righteous prurience of the club reaction, but it does not explain the event itself.

The uncanny occurs in the coincidence of the personal and psychological with the impersonal and metaphysical. What I have called coyness here derives from our uncertainty about how generalizable this experience is. Simply put—does the universe have to be invoked to explain Adela Quested? One answer may be yes, but this is a less grandiose claim than it seems. Making it is simply to insist on the value of human experience, even when that experience resists an easy decoding. The question, as well, points to the degree to which Forster identifies with Adela, not in the sense that she speaks for him, but as her predicament may stand for his. The hairy animal may be Adela's own repressions and fears, the sign of lovelessness, but it possesses a greater symbolic potency in proportion to its refusal to be identified and locked into an allegorical equation. Adela's animal, both as sexuality and ghostly memory, may be the author's, too. And as ghost, the animal works on another textual level; there the writer encounters his own past, his own dead, and the writing itself functions as exorcism.

The motif of exorcism is stated explicitly in a scene after the trial, when Fielding and Adela attempt to account for her "extraordinary behaviour." Fielding speaks first:

> "My belief—and of course I was listening carefully, in hope you would make some slip—my belief is that poor McBryde exorcised you. As soon as he asked you a straightforward question, you gave a straightforward answer and broke down."
> "Exorcise in that sense. I thought you meant I'd seen a ghost."
> "I don't go to that length!"

"People whom I respect very much believe in ghosts," she said rather sharply. "My friend Mrs. Moore does."

"She's an old lady."

"I think you need not be impolite to her, as well as to her son."

"I did not intend to be rude. I only meant it is difficult, as we get on in life, to resist the supernatural. I've felt it coming on me myself. I still jog on without it, but what a temptation, at forty-five, to pretend that the dead live again; one's own dead; no one else's matter."

"Because the dead don't live again."

"I fear not."

"So do I."

There was a moment's silence, such as often follows the triumph of rationalism. (*PI*, 240–41)

What Fielding calls the temptation to make the dead live again is felt at crucial moments inside the text; a passage describing Aziz with the photograph of his dead wife is a good example. The unreal photographic image provides an emblem of her elusiveness: "The very fact that we have loved the dead increases their unreality, and . . . the more passionately we invoke them, the further they recede" (*PI*, 58). This figure of baffled desire has a long literary history that begins with Homer in Achilles' dream of the dead Patroclus and Odysseus's encounter with the shade of his mother and with Virgil in Aeneas's search for the lost Creusa. Forster invokes it within his text, but it resonates beyond the text as well, as it describes the author encountering and exorcising his own ghosts in the act of writing his novel. Santha Rama Rau's description of *The Hill of Devi* in her review of the memoir three decades after *A Passage to India* may be even more pertinent to the novel. *The Hill of Devi* is "a tribute to ghosts," she wrote. "It is a ghostly memory of people who are now dead or in changed positions and to whom Mr. Forster was deeply attached" (*Nation*, 10). In this sense, Adela's exorcism was also Forster's as he attempted to free himself of his own ghosts, especially the ghost of his Alexandrian friend, Mohammed el Adl, who died in May 1922. It was no doubt Mrs. Moore's ghost that followed her ship up the Red Sea, but it may also have been that of Mohammed, who died not very far from that sea.

Of course, such assertions cannot be proved. Fielding's observation "that people are not really dead until they are felt to be dead" (*PI*, 255) certainly explains how Mrs. Moore like Mrs. Wilcox continues to live in the lives of the other characters. But can it be generalized to Forster's own confrontation with his dead? And even if it can, how does that help us as readers of his text? There are extra textual sources that can be invoked in response to the first question. The "Letter-Book to Mohammed" that Forster began several months after Mohammed's death and that he continued to write in during the composition of the novel was an attempt to "write for [his] own comfort and to recall the past."[4] The recall turned out to be impossible. Although the act of writing was an attempt to keep Mohammed alive, the past was rendered unreal by the words used to commemorate it. "This business of remembering a past incident. The horror, beauty, depth, emotional and mental insecurity," he wrote to his friend Joe Ackerley (upon reading Ackerley's poem "Ghosts" in the London Mercury in 1922), reminded him of Proust's use of the Celtic belief that the dead can return. But he doubts this even as he pursues his ghosts. "I don't know whether you and Proust are right in your explanations," the letter continues. " 'Out of death lead no ways'[5] is more probably the fact. What you have done is to drive home the strangeness of a creature who is apparently allowed neither to remember nor to forget. . . . The moment a memory is registered by the intellect is its last moment" (Lago and Furbank, 2:24–25).

For the second question one might remember Forster's claim that he willed his mind to remain a blur when writing the central scene; that is, he put himself in the mental state he described in the letter, neither remembering nor forgetting. The creation of this uncanny space below the threshold of the intellect may have been a biographical as well as a narrative necessity. For the will not to know records both a swerving away from the memory of his own desire (as I argued in discussing the "Kanaya" fragment) and the baffled attempt to make his own dead live again before the final letting go. The reader is conscious of this but only dimly; like the Marabar at dusk it passes by on averted wings, but it leaves enough of a trace to return us to the scene obsessively. What happened? How can we tell? What does it mean? Describing A Passage to India as a ghost story is one way to identify this elusiveness, the essential secrecy of the novel. Very possibly we should not "resist the supernatural" in responding to a text that derives so much of its imaginative power from the shadow world of memory and desire.

Notes

Chapter 1

1. Quoted in Philip Gardner, *E. M. Forster: Critical Heritage* (London: Routledge & Kegan Paul, 1973), 236; hereafter cited in text.

2. "A happy ending was imperative. I shouldn't have bothered to write otherwise. I was determined that in fiction anyway two men should fall in love and remain in it for the ever and ever that fiction allows" ("Terminal Note," in *Maurice* [London: Edward Arnold, 1971], 236).

3. Elizabeth Bowen, "A Passage to E. M. Forster," in *Aspects of E. M. Forster*, ed. Oliver Stallybrass (New York: Harcourt, Brace & World, 1969), 4; hereafter cited in text.

4. Virginia Woolf, *Collected Essays* (London: Hogarth Press, 1966), 2:104; hereafter cited in text.

5. Michael Levenson, *Modernism and the Fate of Individuality* (Cambridge: Cambridge University Press, 1991), 139–40; hereafter cited in text.

6. Forster to Goldsworthy Lowes Dickinson, 8 May 1922, in *Selected Letters of E. M. Forster*, ed. Mary Lago and P. N. Furbank (Cambridge, Mass.: Harvard University Press, 1985), 2:26; hereafter cited in text.

7. *Abinger Harvest* (New York: Harcourt, Brace & World, 1964), 113; hereafter cited in text as *AH*.

8. David Lodge, *Working with Structuralism* (London: Routledge & Kegan Paul, 1981), 6.

9. 12 February 1927, *The Diary of Virginia Woolf*, ed. A. O. Bell (New York: Harcourt Brace Jovanovich, 1980), 3:127.

10. See Perry Meisel, *The Myth of the Modern: A Study in British Literature and Criticism after 1850* (New Haven: Yale University Press, 1987), for an account of the problem of origins for writers "coming late in a tradition" (2), when "neither writers nor readers are originals, nor are their materials; each is constituted in a vortex of tradition in which belatedness is both the precondition and the acknowledged dynamic of writing and reading alike" (73).

11. P. N. Furbank, *E. M. Forster: A Life* (London: Secker & Warburg, 1977, 1978), 2:163; hereafter cited in text.

12. Wyndham Lewis, in Jo Anna Isaak, *The Ruin of Representation in Modernist Art and Texts* (Ann Arbor: UMI Research Press, 1986), 9.

13. G. E. Moore, *Principia Ethica* (Cambridge: Cambridge University Press, 1922), 88.

14. Ezra Pound, *Personae: The Shorter Poems of Ezra Pound*, ed. Lea Baechler and A. Walton Litz (New York: New Directions, 1990), 186.

15. D. Fokkema and E. Ibsch, *Modernist Conjectures* (New York: St. Martin's Press, 1988), 34–47.

Chapter 2

1. *Two Cheers for Democracy*, Abinger Edition no. 11 (London: Edward Arnold, 1972), 265.

2. In his notes to the 1942 Everyman edition of *A Passage to India* Forster wrote: "I have not tried to correct errors in fact, which must be plentiful, especially in chapter 24, nor to indicate anachronisms, such as my uses of 'Lieutenant-Governor' and of 'Anglo-Indian.' " Quoted in *A Passage to India*, Abinger Edition no. 6 (London: Edward Arnold, 1978), 346; hereafter cited in text as *Ab. PI.*

3. Percival Spear, "The Mughals and the British," in *A Cultural History of India*, ed. A. L. Basham (Oxford: Clarendon Press, 1975), 352; hereafter cited in text.

4. According to *Hobson-Jobson: A Glossary of Colloquial Anglo-Indian Words and Phrases*, "it began to be applied in the 18th century, when the transactions of Clive [Robert, Baron Clive of Plassey] made the epithet familiar in England, to Anglo-Indians who returned with fortunes from the East" (610). This wonderful dictionary compiled by H. Yule and A. C. Burnell was first published in 1886 and has since gone frequently in and out of print. Reprinted by Rupa & Co., Calcutta, 1986.

5. F. Braudel, *The Wheels of Commerce* (London: Collins, 1982), 222.

6. Thomas Babington Macaulay, *Selected Writings*, ed. J. L. Clive and T. Pinney (Chicago: University of Chicago Press, 1972), 241; see Edward Said, *Orientalism* (New York: Pantheon, 1978) for an exposition and critique of Orientalism.

7. "*The Art and Architecture of India* by Benjamin Rowland," *Listener* (London), 10 September 1953, 419–21.

8. Quoted by Jonathan Arac in "Tradition, Discipline, and Trouble," in *Profession 90* (New York: Modern Language Association, 1990), 15.

9. Quoted by Benita Parry in *Delusions and Discoveries* (Berkeley: University of California Press, 1972), 15; see also G. K. Das, *E. M. Forster's India* (London: Macmillan Press, 1977), 24; both hereafter cited in text.

10. Quoted by Patrick Brantlinger in *Rule of Darkness* (Ithaca: Cornell University Press, 1988), 202; hereafter cited in text.

11. Quoted by Lewis Wurgaft in *The Imperial Imagination: Magic and Myth in Kipling's India* (Middletown, Conn.: Wesleyan University Press, 1983), 23; hereafter cited in text.

12. N. S. Bose, *The Indian National Movement* (Calcutta: Firma K. L. Mukhopadhyah, 1974), 76.

13. Aziz Ahmad, "Islamic Reform Movements," in Basham, *A Cultural History of India*, 389.

14. Quoted by S. R. Mehrotra in *Towards India's Freedom and Partition* (New Delhi: Vikas Publishing House, 1979), 169.

15. M. M. Mahood, "Amritsar to Chandrapore: E. M. Forster and the Massacre," *Encounter* 41 (September 1973): 27; see also G. K. Das, "A Passage to India: A Socio-historical Study," in *A Passage to India: Essays in Interpretation*, ed. J. Beer (London: Macmillan Press, 1985); hereafter cited in text as Beer 1985.

16. *The Hill of Devi*, Abinger edition no. 14 (London: Edward Arnold, 1983), viii; hereafter cited in text as *Hill*. The volume also contains Forster's unpublished letters and journals.

17. *Nation*, 14 November 1953, 408; hereafter cited in text.

18. Robin J. Lewis, *E. M. Forster's Passages to India* (New York: Columbia University Press, 1979), 50.

19. *A Passage to India* (New York: Harcourt Brace Jovanich, Harvest Books, 1965), 80; hereafter cited in text as *PI*.

20. *Pharos and Pharillon* (London: Hogarth Press, 1923), 91; hereafter cited in text as *PP*.

21. Jane Lagoudis Pinchin, *Alexandria Still: Forster, Durrell, and Cavafy* (Princeton, N.J.: Princeton University Press, 1977), 146.

22. Forster to Florence Barger, 7 July 1922; the letter is at King's College, Cambridge.

23. *The Government of Egypt, with Notes on Egypt by EMF* (London: Labour Research Department, 1920), 6; hereafter cited in text as *Egypt*.

24. The undated letter is in the Berg Collection of the New York Public Library.

25. *Writers at Work: The Paris Review Interviews*, ed. Kay Dick (Harmondsworth: Penguin Books, 1972), 10; hereafter cited in text as *Paris Review*.

26. Forster to Syed Ross Masood, 27 September 1922; the letter is at King's College, Cambridge.

Chapter 3

1. Term used to denote the British rule in India until independence in 1947.

2. *E. M. Forster: A Tribute*, ed. K. Natwar-Singh (New York: Harcourt, Brace World, 1964), 56; hereafter in text.

3. J. S. Herz and R. K. Martin, eds., *E. M. Forster: Centenary Revaluations* (London: Macmillan Press, 1982), 291–92.

4. Christopher Isherwood, *Lions and Shadows* (London: New English Library, 1974), 107.

5. Benita Parry, "A Passage to India: Epitaph or Manifesto," in *E. M. Forster: A Human Exploration*, ed. G. K. Das and John Beer (London: Macmillan Press, 1979), 140; hereafter cited in text.

6. *The Collected Poetry of W. H. Auden* (New York: Random House, 1945), 53.

7. *Aspects of the Novel*, Abinger Edition no. 12 (London: Edward Arnold, 1978), 169; hereafter cited in text as *AN*.

Chapter 4

1. B. J. Kirkpatrick, *A Bibliography of E. M. Forster*, Soho Bibliographies no. 19, 2d ed. (Oxford: Clarendon Press, 1985), 32–34.

2. Derek Traversi, "The Novels of E. M. Forster," *Arena* 1 (1937): 28–40; Austin Warren, "The Novels of E. M. Forster," *American Review* 9 (1937): 226–51.

3. Lionel Trilling, *E. M. Forster* (Norfolk, Conn.: New Directions, 1943), 144. Unless otherwise indicated, the books and articles subsequently referred to in this chapter are listed with full publication information in the bibliography.

4. Peter Burra's essay was reprinted again in the Abinger Edition of *A Passage to India*, 315–27.

5. *Literary History of England*, ed. Albert Baugh (New York: Appleton Century Crofts, 1948), 1569.

6. Nirad Chaudhuri, "Passage to and from India," *Encounter* 2 (1954): 19–24.

7. Andrew Shonfield, "The Politics of Forster's India," *Encounter* 30 (1968): 62–69; David Shusterman, *The Quest for Certitude* (Bloomington: University of Indiana Press, 1965), 182–202.

8. L. Dauner, "What Happened in the Cave?" *Modern Fiction Studies* 7 (1961): 258–70.

9. Wilfred Stone, *The Cave and the Mountain* (Stanford, Calif.: Stanford University Press, 1966), 339; hereafter cited in text.

Chapter 5

1. Edmund Candler, *Abdication* (London: Constable, 1922), 136.

2. A. JanMohammed, "The Economy of Manichean Allegory: The Function of Racial Difference in Colonialist Literature," *Critical Inquiry* 12 (1985): 59–87, is a very carefully argued example.

3. Nirad Chaudhuri, "On Understanding the Hindus," *Encounter* 24 (1965): 24.

4. See Allen Greenberger, *The British Image of India* (London: Oxford University Press, 1969), 128; and Parry 1972, 47.

5. Flora Annie Steel, *The Law of the Threshold* (New York: Macmillan, 1924), 1; hereafter cited in text.

6. S. V. Pradhan, "Anglo Indian Fiction and E. M. Forster," *New Quest* (Poona, India) 1 (1977): 19.

Notes

7. Rudyard Kipling, *Kim* (London: Macmillan, 1901), 258.

8. Frances Singh, "*A Passage to India*, the National Movement, and Independence," *Twentieth Century Literature* 31 (1985): 274; hereafter cited in text.

9. Quoted by J. Meyers, "The Politics of *A Passage to India*," *Journal of Modern Literature* 1 (1971): 336.

10. "Three Countries," in *The Hill of Devi*, 298.

11. See the summary in June Perry Levine, *Creation and Criticism* (Lincoln: University of Nebraska Press, 1971), 128–39.

12. E. K. Brown, *Rhythm in the Novel* (Toronto: University of Toronto Press, 1950), 113.

13. Walt Whitman, "Passage to India," in *Leaves of Grass, Comprehensive Reader's Edition*, ed. H. W. Blodgett and S. Bradley (New York: New York University Press, 1965), p. 412, ll. 121–23; hereafter cited in text.

14. Forster to Josie Darling, 20 June 1915; the letter is at King's College, Cambridge.

Chapter 6

1. Jorge Luis Borges, "Pierre Menard, Author of the *Quixote*," in *Labyrinths* (New York: New Directions, 1964), 36–44.

2. Kenneth Burke, "Social and Cosmic Mystery: *A Passage to India*," in *Language as Symbolic Action* (Berkeley: University of California Press, 1966), 226.

3. Malcolm Bradbury, "Two Passages to India: Forster as Victorian and Modern," in Natwar-Singh, 141.

4. Bradbury makes the comparison central to his argument; see also M. Ragussis, *The Subterfuge of Art: Language and the Romantic Tradition* (Baltimore: Johns Hopkins University Press, 1978), 142; D. Dowling, "*A Passage to India* through 'the Spaces between the Words,'" *Journal of Narrative Technique* 15 (1985): 256.

Chapter 7

1. G. Genette, *Narrative Discourse: An Essay in Method*, trans. J. Lewin (Ithaca, N.Y.: Cornell University Press, 1980), 189–98, and *Narrative Discourse Revisited* (Ithaca, N.Y.: Cornell University Press, 1988); M. Bal, "The Narrating and the Focalizing," *Style* 17 (1983): 234–69; S. Rimmon-Kenan, *Narrative Fiction: Contemporary Poetics* (London: Methuen, 1983), 71–85.

2. Rimmon-Kenan, 73; hereafter cited in text. Her discussion of *Great Expectations* makes clear that the narrator/focalizer distinction also holds for first-person narratives.

3. See Brenda Silver, "Periphrasis, Power, Rape in *A Passage to India*," *Novel* 22 (1988): 95; for its theoretical context see Eve Kosofsky Sedgwick, *Between Men: English Literature and Male Homosocial Desire* (New York: Columbia University Press, 1985), 25–26, and Luce Irigaray, "Women on the

Market," in *This Sex Which Is Not One*, trans. C. Porter (Ithaca, N.Y.: Cornell University Press, 1985), 172; for the photograph, see Francesca Kazan, "Confabulations in *A Passage to India*," *Criticism* 29 (1987): 204ff.

4. John Colmer, *E. M. Forster: The Personal Voice* (London: Routledge & Kegan Paul, 1975), 168.

5. Michael Orange, "Language and Silence in *A Passage to India*," in Das and Beer, 157.

6. *The Manuscripts of "A Passage to India*," Abinger Edition 6a, ed. O. Stallybrass, (London: Edward Arnold, 1978), 144; hereafter cited in text as *Mss.* This volume reprints the available manuscript fragments of the different stages of the novel's evolution.

7. Foreword to *Flowers and Elephants*, by Constance Sitwell (London: Jonathan Cape, 1927), ii; hereafter cited in text.

8. Roger Ebbatson and Catherine Neale, *E. M. Forster: A Passage to India* (Harmondsworth: Penguin Books, 1986) 62; hereafter cited in text.

Chapter 8

1. For example, in Kipling's *Naulahka* (written with Wolcott Balestier) and Conrad's *Heart of Darkness*. See S. Cooperman, "The Imperial Posture and the Shrine of Darkness," *ELT* 6 (1963): 9–13; and D. A. Shankar, "The *Naulahka* and Post-Kipling British Fiction," *Literary Criterion* (Mysore) 22 (1987): 71–79; see also Wurgaft, 51–53, 136–38.

2. Some critics have argued, in contrast to the position I am taking here, that the reader is allowed to assume that a rape may have occurred. See Frances Restuccia, for example, " 'A Cave of My Own': E. M. Forster and Sexual Politics," *Raritan* 9 (1989), where Aziz is viewed as "neither indictable nor exculpable," with the result that indeterminacy becomes a cover for misogyny (114, 118). For the argument that it was an angered guard, an adherent of the Jain religion, see J. Moran, "E. M. Forster's *A Passage to India*: What Really Happened in the Caves," *Modern Fiction Studies* 34 (1988): 596–604.

3. F. Kermode, "Endings, Continued," in *Languages of the Unsayable*, ed. S. Budick and W. Iser (New York: Columbia University Press, 1989), 75.

4. Gillian Beer, "Negation in *A Passage to India*," *Essays in Criticism* 30 (1980): 151–66; rptd. in John Beer 1985, 54.

5. A. N. Upadhye, "Jainism," in Basham, 105.

6. Avrom Fleishman, "Being and Nothing in *A Passage to India*," in *Fiction and the Ways of Knowing* (Austin: University of Texas Press, 1978), 149–62.

7. Gillian Beer in Beer 1985, 156, develops these puns; also see Jeffrey Heath, "A Voluntary Surrender: Imperialism and Imagination in *A Passage to India*," *University of Toronto Quarterly* 59 (1989): 303.

8. See Kazan, "Confabulations in *A Passage to India*," 200.

Notes

Chapter 9

1. Elaine Showalter, "*A Passage to India* as Marriage Fiction," *Women and Literature* 5 (1977): 14.

2. Forster to Syed Ross Masood, 9 September 1923; the letter is at King's College, Cambridge.

Chapter 10

1. *Alexandria: A History and a Guide* (New York: Doubleday, 1961), 71.

2. R. Brower, *The Fields of Light* (New York: Oxford University Press, 1951), 197.

3. Alan Wilde, "Modernism and the Aesthetics of Crisis," *Contemporary Literature* 20 (1979): 16.

Chapter 11

1. "The Gods of India," in *Albergo Empedocle and Other Writings*, ed. George Thomson (New York: Liveright, 1971), 223.

2. S. Freud, "The Uncanny," trans. James Strachey, rptd. in *New Literary History* 7 (1976): 623; hereafter cited in text. It is unlikely that Forster would have read the essay when it was first published in German in 1919, but the model Freud developed, using Schelling's description of the uncanny and E. T. A. Hoffmann's story "The Sandman," is illuminating for Forster's practice.

3. O. Mannoni, *Prospero and Caliban: The Psychology of Colonialism* (New York: Praeger, 1964), 20.

4. August 1922–December 1929; the manuscript is at King's College, Cambridge.

5. Forster is quoting a poem of Thomas Love Beddoes: "Out of death lead no ways / There are no ghosts to raise / Vain is the call." See note in Lago and Furbank, 2:25.

Bibliography

With very few exceptions, all entries relating to Forster in this bibliography are annotated in the bibliographies of F. P. W. McDowell (1976) and C. Summers (1991). Other items have been included for their pertinence to my reading and are discussed in the text.

PRIMARY WORKS

The Hill of Devi and Other Indian Writings. Edited by Elizabeth Heine. Abinger Edition no. 14. London: Edward Arnold, 1983.

The Manuscripts of "A Passage to India." Edited by Oliver Stallybrass. Abinger Edition no. 6A. London: Edward Arnold, 1978.

A Passage to India. New York: Harcourt Brace Jovanovich, 1965.

A Passage to India. Edited by Oliver Stallybrass. Abinger Edition no. 6. London: Edward Arnold, 1978.

Selected Letters of E. M. Forster. Edited by Mary Lago and P. N. Furbank. Cambridge, Mass.: Harvard University Press, 1985.

SECONDARY WORKS

Biographies and Bibliographies

Furbank, P. N. *E. M. Forster: A Life.* London: Secker & Warburg, 1977. Reprint, 1978.

Gardner, Philip. *E. M. Forster: The Critical Heritage.* London: Routledge & Kegan Paul, 1973.

Kirkpatrick, B. J. *A Bibliography of E. M. Forster.* 2d ed. Soho Bibliographies no. 19. Oxford: Clarendon Press, 1985.

McDowell, Frederick P. W. *E. M. Forster: An Annotated Bibliography of Writings about Him.* DeKalb: Northern Illinois University Press, 1976.

Stape, J. H. *An E. M. Forster Chronology.* London: Macmillan Press, 1992.

Summers, Claude J. *E. M. Forster: A Guide to Research.* New York: Garland, 1991.

Criticism: Books and Parts of Books

Beer, Gillian. "Negation in *A Passage to India.*" In *A Passage to India: Essays in Interpretation,* edited by John Beer, 44–58. London: Macmillan Press, 1985.

Beer, John. *The Achievement of E. M. Forster.* London: Chatto & Windus, 1962.

_____. *"A Passage to India": Essays in Interpretation.* London: Macmillan Press, 1985.

_____. *"A Passage to India:* The French New Novel and English Romanticism." In *E. M. Forster: Centenary Revaluations,* edited by Judith Scherer Herz and Robert K. Martin, 124–52. London: Macmillan Press, 1982.

Bradbury, Malcolm, ed. *Forster: A Collection of Critical Essays.* Englewood Cliffs, N.J.: Prentice-Hall, 1966.

_____. "Two Passages to India: Forster as Victorian and Modern." In *Aspects of E. M. Forster,* edited by Oliver Stallybrass. London: Edward Arnold, 1969.

Brantlinger, Patrick. *Rule of Darkness: British Literature and Imperialism, 1830–1914.* Ithaca, N.Y.: Cornell University Press, 1988.

Burke, Kenneth. "Social and Cosmic Mystery: *A Passage to India.*" *Language as Symbolic Action: Essays on Life, Literature, and Method.* Berkeley: University of California Press, 1967.

Colmer, John. *E. M. Forster: "A Passage to India."* London: Edward Arnold, 1967.

_____. *E. M. Forster: The Personal Voice.* London: Routledge & Kegan Paul, 1975.

Crews, Frederick. *E. M. Forster: The Perils of Humanism.* Princeton, N.J.: Princeton University Press, 1962.

Das, G. K. *E. M. Forster's India.* London: Macmillan Press, 1977.

_____. "E. M. Forster and Hindu Mythology." In *E. M. Forster: Centenary Revolutions,* edited by Judith Scherer Herz and Robert K. Martin, 244–56. London: Macmillan Press, 1982.

_____. *"A Passage to India:* A Socio-historical Study." In *A Passage to India: Essays in Interpretation,* edited by John Beer, 1985, 1–15. London: Macmillan Press, 1985.

_____, and Beer, John. *E. M. Forster: A Human Exploration.* London: Macmillan, 1979.

Ebbatson, R., and Neale, C. *E. M. Forster: "A Passage to India."* Penguin Critical Studies. Harmondsworth: Penguin Books, 1986. Reprint, 1989.

Finkelstein, Bonnie Blumenthal. *Forster's Women: Eternal Differences.* New York: Columbia University Press, 1975.

Fleishman, Avrom. "Being and Nothing in *A Passage to India.*" In *Fiction and the Ways of Knowing: Essays on British Novels.* Austin: University of Texas Press, 1978.

Grandsen, K. W. *E. M. Forster.* Edinburgh and London: Oliver & Boyd, 1962. Rev. ed., 1970.

Greenberger, Alan J. *The British Image of India: A Study in the Literature of Imperialism 1880–1960.* London: Oxford University Press, 1969.

Bibliography

Herz, Judith Scherer, and Martin, Robert K. *E. M. Forster: Centenary Revaluations.* London: Macmillan Press, 1982.

Levenson, Michael. *Modernism and the Fate of Individuality: Character and Novelistic Form from Conrad to Woolf.* Cambridge: Cambridge University Press, 1991.

Levine, June Perry. *Creation and Criticism: "A Passage to India."* Lincoln: University of Nebraska Press, 1971.

Lewis, Robin J. *E. M. Forster's Passages to India.* New York: Columbia University Press, 1979.

London, Bette. *The Appropriated Voice: Narrative Authority in Conrad, Forster, and Woolf.* Ann Arbor: University of Michigan Press, 1990.

McConkey, James. *The Novels of E. M. Forster.* Ithaca, N.Y.: Cornell University Press, 1957.

McDowell, Frederick P. W. *E. M. Forster: Revised Edition.* Boston: Twayne, 1982.

Mannoni, O. *Prospero and Caliban: The Psychology of Colonialism.* New York: Praeger, 1964.

Meisel, Perry. *The Myth of the Modern: A Study in British Literature and Criticism after 1850.* New Haven, Conn.: Yale University Press, 1987.

Natwar-Singh, K., ed. *E. M. Forster: A Tribute with Selections from His Writings on India.* New York: Harcourt, Brace & World, 1964.

Orange, Michael. "Language and Silence in *A Passage to India.*" In Das and Beer, 1979.

Parry, Benita. *Delusions and Discoveries: Studies on India in the British Imagination.* Berkeley: University of California Press, 1972.

_____. "*A Passage to India:* Epitaph or Manifesto?" In Das and Beer, 1979, and Wilde, 1985.

_____. "The Politics of Representation in *A Passage to India.*" In Beer, 1985.

Pinchin, Jane Lagoudis. *Alexandria Still: Forster, Durrell, and Cavafy.* Princeton, N.J.: Princeton University Press, 1977.

Quinones, R.; Chefdor M.; and Wachtel, A. *Modernism: Challenges and Perspectives.* Chicago: University of Chicago Press, 1986.

Rosecrance, Barbara. *Forster's Narrative Vision.* Ithaca, N.Y.: Cornell University Press, 1982.

Rosenbaum, S. P., ed. *The Bloomsbury Group: A Collection of Memoirs, Commentary, and Criticism.* Toronto: University of Toronto Press, 1975.

Said, Edward. *Orientalism.* New York: Random House, 1978.

Stallybrass, Oliver, ed. *Aspects of E. M. Forster: Essays and Recollections Written for His Ninetieth Birthday.* New York: Harcourt, Brace & World, 1969.

_____. "Forster's Wobblings: The Manuscripts of *A Passage to India.*" In Stallybrass, 1969.

Stone, Wilfred. *The Cave and the Mountain: A Study of E. M. Forster.* Stanford, Calif.: Stanford University Press, 1966.

Summers, Claude. *E. M. Forster: Literature and Life.* New York: Ungar, 1983.

Thomson, George. *The Fiction of E. M. Forster.* Detroit: Wayne State University Press, 1967.

Trilling, Lionel. *E. M. Forster.* New York: New Directions, 1943.

Wilde, Alan. *Art and Order: A Study of E. M. Forster.* New York: New York University Press, 1964.

_____, ed. *Critical Essays on E. M. Forster.* Boston: G. K. Hall, 1985.

Wurgaft, Lewis. *The Imperial Imagination: Magic and Myth in Kipling's India.* Middletown, Conn., Wesleyan University Press, 1983.

Yule, H., and Burnell, A. C. *Hobson-Jobson: A Glossary of Colloquial Anglo-Indian Words and Phrases, and of Kindred Terms, Etymological, Historical, Geographical and Discursive* (1886). Calcutta, Allahabad, Bombay, Delhi: Rupa, 1986.

Criticism: Articles

Bodenheimer, Rosemarie. "The Romantic Impasse in *A Passage to India.*" *Criticism* 22 (1980): 40–56.

Conradi, Peter. "The Metaphysical Hostess: The Cult of Personal Relations in the Modern English Novel." *ELH* 48 (1981): 427–53.

Hawkins, Hunt. "Forster's Critique of Imperialism in *A Passage to India.*" *South Atlantic Review* 48 (1983): 54–65.   +PBI S69

Heath, Jeffrey. "A Voluntary Surrender: Imperialism and Imagination in *A Passage to India.*" *University of Toronto Quarterly* 59 (1989–90): 287–309.

JanMohammed, Abdul. "The Economy of Manichean Allegory: The Function of Racial Difference in Colonialist Literature." *Critical Inquiry* 12 (1985): 59–87.

Kazan, Francesca. "Confabulations in *A Passage to India.*" *Criticism* 29 (1987): 197–214.

Meyers, Jeffrey. "The Politics of *A Passage to India.*" *Journal of Modern Literature* 1 (1971): 329–38.

Price, Martin. "People of the Book: Character in Forster's *A Passage to India.*" *Critical Inquiry* 1 (1975): 605–22.   NXI C93

Restuccia, Frances. " 'A Cave of my Own': E. M. Forster and Sexual Politics." *Raritan* 9 (1989): 110–28.   AS30 R22

Sharpe, Jenny. "The Unspeakable Limits of Rape: Colonial Violence and Counter-Insurgency." *Genders* 10 (1991): 25–46.

Showalter, Elaine. "*A Passage to India* as 'Marriage Fiction': Forster's Sexual Politics." *Women and Literature* 5 (1977): 3–16.   PN471 |W8

Silver, Brenda. "Periphrasis, Power, and Rape in *A Passage to India.*" *Novel* 22 (1988): 86–105.

Singh, Frances. "*A Passage to India* the National Movement, and Independence." *Twentieth Century Literature* 31 (1985): 265–78.   PN2 T97

Wilde, Alan. "Modernism and the Aesthetics of Crisis." *Contemporary Literature* 20 (1979): 13–50.

Index

Abinger Harvest, 36
"about," 67–68, 114
Ackerley, Joe, 134
Adl, Mohammed el, 26, 133
Akbar, 13
Albergo Empedocle and Other Writings, 128
Alexandria, 25–26
Alexandria, 3, 25, 116
Ali brothers (Muhammed and Shauket), 20, 22, 55
Aligarh, University of, 11, 21
Amritsar Massacre, 19, 48, 51, 52, 54, 55, 107
Anand, Mulk Raj, 31–32, 33
Anglo-Indian, 13, 17, 22, 45–46, 51, 52, 52–53, 81, 95, 96, 116, 118, 121, 122, 132
Anti-imperialism. *See* Imperialism
Arctic Summer, 24
Aspects of the Novel, 34, 37, 58, 68–69
Auden, W. H., 34
Austen, Jane, 4, 9, 34, 91

babu, 53
Babur, Emperor, 13, 93, 96, 103
Bal, Mieke, 74
Barabar Caves, 23
Barger, Florence, 26
Beer, Gillian, 97
Beer, John, 39
Bengal, partition of, 18
Bennett, Arnold, 4, 5
Bentinck, Lord William, 15
Blast, 8
Bloomsbury, 8

Borges, Jorge Luis, 68
Bose, N. S., 18
Bowen, Elizabeth, 4, 34
Bradbury, Malcolm, 16
Brontë, Emily, 69
Brown, E. K., 37, 58–59
Burke, Kenneth, 68
Burra, Peter, 36, 63

Cambridge, 11, 20, 21, 33, 34, 55, 117
Candler, Edmund, 22, 45, 47
Cavafy, C. P., 25, 26
Cawnpore (Kanpur). *See* Mutiny
Celestial Omnibus, 4, 32
Characters in *A Passage to India*
    Dr. Aziz, 12, 13, 21, 26, 34, 37, 41, 45, 50, 52, 54, 55–56, 63, 64–65, 68, 74, 79, 83–85, 91, 93 94–95, 96, 99, 101, 103, 104, 109, 110, 111, 115, 118, 119, 120–21, 122–23, 124, 125, 126, 130, 131, 132, 133
    Major Callendar, 63, 64, 65
    Mr. Das, 55–56, 59
    Miss Derek, 81, 105
    Fielding, 26, 34, 41, 46, 50, 55, 66, 68, 73, 74, 79, 83, 85–86, 87, 91–96, 101, 103, 104–5, 106, 111, 115–16, 118–19, 121–22, 123–26, 128, 129, 132–33
    Godbole, 23–24, 34, 37–38, 48, 73, 74, 79, 83, 86, 87, 91, 93, 106, 107, 115, 116, 118, 120, 121

Mr. Graysford and Mr. Sorley, 70–71, 80
Hamidullah, 47, 96, 115–16
Heaslop, Ronny, 49, 51, 64, 65–66, 75–80, 81, 92–93, 109, 122, 128, 130
Mr. McBryde, 108, 132
Mrs. McBryde, 105, 108
Mrs. Moore, 26, 35–36, 39, 41, 49, 50, 52, 55, 59, 64–65, 68, 73, 74, 75–79, 81–82, 85, 93–94, 96, 106, 108, 109–11, 114-17, 119, 121, 122–23, 124, 128, 133
Moore, Ralph, 115, 121, 122–23, 126, 128
Moore, Stella, 121, 122, 128
Nawab, Bahadur, 13, 80–81, 96, 128
Punkah wallah, 108–9, 123
Quested, Adela, 27, 48, 49, 50, 52, 64, 65–66, 68, 81, 87, 91, 92–93, 94, 95, 96–97, 99, 101, 103, 105–11, 119, 120, 128, 129, 130, 132–33
Mr. Turton, 69, 79, 108
Mrs. Turton, 50, 51, 52, 108
Chaudhuri, Nirad, 37, 47–48
Chhatarpur, Maharajah of, 23
Christianity, 62, 79, 94, 119–20
Collected Short Stories, 37
Colmer, John, 40, 86
Colonialism, postcolonialism, 31, 39, 40, 41, 46, 57, 65, 94, 99–100, 104, 122, 132
Conrad, Joseph, 4, 5, 69
Crews, Frederick, 38
"The Curate's Friend," 91

Darling, Josie, 59–60
Darling, Malcolm, 21, 25
Das, G. K., 40, 54
Dauner, Louise, 38
Derrida, Jacques, 97
Dewas Senior, Rajah of, 21–22, 23, 27
Dewas, court of, 23, 56, 100–101
Dickinson, Goldsworthy Lowes, 36, 82

Disraeli, Benjamin, 16, 17
Diver, Maud, 49, 95
Duncan, Sara Jeanette, 22
Dyarchy, 18, 19
Dyer, General Reginald, 19, 52

East India Company, 12, 14
Ebbatson, R., 88, 89
Eliot, T. S., 8–9
    The Waste Land, 5, 9, 124
Egypt, 26–27, 78
Ellora, Buddhist caves at, 23
Eurasian, 13, 61

Fabian Society, 26
Fantasy, the fantastic, 4, 32, 33, 34
Finkelstein, Bonnie, 41
Flowers and Elephants, Forster's foreword to, 87, 104
Focalization, 74, 75, 77, 79, 95, 103–4, 120
Free indirect discourse, 75–82, 104
Freud, Sigmund ("The Uncanny"), 129–30
Fry, Roger, 7, 8
Furbank, P. N., 7, 40

Gandhi, 19, 20, 27, 45, 54–55, 56
Galsworthy, John, 4, 5
Genette, Gérard, 74
Ghosts, 22, 25, 26, 73, 85, 89, 111, 115, 127–34
Gokul, Ashtami, 28, 123
Government of India Acts, 12, 18
Grandsen, K. W., 38

Hartal, 19
Hartley, L. P., 35
Heine, Elizabeth, 28, 40
The Hill of Devi, 21–22, 23, 27–28, 37, 56, 133
Hinduism, 37–38, 39, 57–58, 109, 113, 115–16, 119–20, 123, 128
Hindu/Muslim entente, 18, 20, 37–38, 48, 54, 55–56, 108
Homer, 133

Homosexuality, 3–4, 25, 26
Howards End, 4, 20, 21, 24, 32, 33, 115, 117
Humanism. *See* Liberal humanism

Imperialism, anti-imperialism, 26, 41, 56, 57, 100, 104
Indian Civil Service, 13, 17, 21, 51, 64
Indian National Congress, 11, 17–18, 20, 54, 124
Influenza, epidemic of 1919, 19
Isherwood, Christopher, 32–33
Iyer, Raghavan, 16

Jainism, 39, 97–98, 117
James, Henry, 4, 5, 37, 75
JanMohamed, A., 39
Joyce, James, 5, 8, 75

Kali, 53, 117
"Kanaya Memoir," 28, 100–101, 134
Kermode, Frank, 31, 97
Khan, Sir Syed Ahmed, 11, 21
Khilifat movement, 20, 54
Krishna, 28, 34, 58, 86, 116, 118, 123

Lago, Mary, 7, 40
Language, 15, 66–67, 83, 89, 108, 109–10
   lingo, 50, 79–80
Lawrence, D. H., 5, 6–7, 69
"The Letter-book to Mohammed," 134
Levenson, Michael, 5
Lewis, Robin, 24, 40
Lewis, Wyndham, 8
Liberal humanism, 34, 38, 40, 55
"The Life to Come," 40
Lodge, David, 6
London, Bette, 40–41
The Longest Journey, 20, 32, 117

Macaulay, Rose, 36
Macaulay, Thomas Babington, 15–16
McConkey, James, 37, 40

McDowell, F. P. N., 39
Mannoni, O., 132
Maratha Confederacy, 13, 14
Marianne Thornton, 37
Marriage, 25, 59, 63–64, 66, 67
Masood, Syed Ross, 11, 20–21, 22, 25, 60, 107
Maurice, 3–4, 25, 33, 40
Melville, Herman, 34, 69
   Moby-Dick, 9, 69
Minto-Morley India Councils Act, 18
Modernism, 4, 6, 7–8, 9, 33, 126
Mogul Empire, 13–14
Mohurram, 107, 123
Moore, G. E., 8
Montagu-Chelmsford reforms, 18
Motifs and themes in *A Passage to India*
   boum, 81, 89, 93–94, 99, 129
   the collar stud, 92, 119, 120
   double vision, 60, 81, 110, 114, 129
   the echo, 52, 58, 82, 85, 89, 93–94, 96, 101, 105–6, 107, 110, 117, 128, 129, 131
   exorcism, 132–33
   the field glasses, 92–93, 96
   fists and fingers, 62, 97, 105, 117
   friendship, 55, 86, 91, 92, 95, 100, 110, 115, 118, 124–25, 127
   "God is love," 119
   hospitality, 50, 64, 70, 93, 103
   the hyena, 97, 109, 130, 131
   improvisation, 93–95
   inclusion/exclusion, 32, 60, 66, 68, 69, 70–71, 116, 120, 123–25
   India as woman, 60, 94–95
   invitation, 49, 64, 65, 69–70, 71, 80, 91–92, 103
   metaphysical horror, 85, 94, 96
   nothing, 58, 61, 70, 73, 80, 89, 91, 92, 94, 98, 99, 110, 114, 125, 127–28
   the photograph, 85–86, 129, 133

"the real India," 51, 66
"seeing India," 51, 111
· sexual fear, 94–95, 96, 131
silence, 73, 85, 86–87, 88, 89,
104, 108
stones, 71, 89, 96, 97, 106
the unknown bird, 87, 88, 131
the wasp, 66, 70, 84, 89, 116,
119
Mukherjee, Bharati, 32
Murry, John Middleton, 35
Muslim League, 18, 20
Muslim revival, 11, 22
Muslim Young Party, 54
Muslims, attitudes toward, 47–48,
51, 53–54, 84
Mutiny of 1857, 12, 16–17, 19–20,
52

Nabob, 14
Narrative theory, 68, 71, 73, 74
Narrator, 50, 64, 69, 70–71, 73,
74, 75–78, 79, 81, 83, 87,
95–96, 103, 118, 120, 126,
128, 129
Neale, C., 88–89
Nehru, Jawaharal, 95
Non-Cooperation movement, 20,
54, 55, 56, 108

O'Dwyer, Michael, 51
Orange, Michael, 86

A Passage to India. See also
Characters; Motifs and
themes; Places and scenes
early versions in manuscript,
27, 29, 98–99, 107, 109
film, 109
Parry, Benita, 34, 39, 89
Pharos and Pharillon, 3, 4, 26
Pinchin, Jane Lagoudis, 26
Places and scenes in A Passage to
India
the accident on the Marabar
Road, 80, 96, 109, 130
the birth of Krishna, 28, 58,
116, 120, 122–23

the Bridge Party, 49, 50, 52, 66,
69, 75, 76, 91, 111
the caves, 23, 24, 37, 58, 66, 82,
91, 92, 93–101, 107, 110,
129–30
Chandrapore, 12, 22
the club, 48–52, 64–67
the courtroom, 23, 57, 71, 80,
93, 94, 96, 99, 103–11
the expedition to the caves, 86,
92–95, 104–5, 107
Fielding's tea party, 86, 88, 91,
111, 118
Kawa Dol, 99, 118
the last ride, 34, 123
the Marabar Hills, 61–62, 91,
105, 125, 129, 134
Mau, 23, 94, 120–21, 125
the mosque, 37, 64–66, 83, 111,
115
Plassey, British defeat at, 14
Point of view, 46, 55–56, 63,
74–75, 78, 81, 82, 84, 87, 99,
120. See also Focalization
Pound, Ezra, 5, 8, 9
Prophecy, 34, 68–69
Proust, Marcel, 5, 34, 37, 134

the Raj, 11–29, 31
Ransom, J. C., 37
Rape, 41, 76, 94–95, 99–100
Rau, Santha Rama, 22, 31, 59,
114–15, 133
Realism, 4, 6, 32, 36, 68, 73, 76,
87–88, 92–93, 104, 107, 109,
119
Regulating Acts (1773), 14, 15
Restuccia, Frances, 41
Rimmon-Kenan, Shlomith, 74–75
A Room with a View, 4, 20, 32
Rosecrance, Barbara, 40
Rowlatt Acts (1919), 19, 55, 108,
109
Roy, Ram Mohan, 15

Sahib, Nana, 16
Salisbury, Robert, 17
Satyagraha, 19

Saville, Sir George, 14
Sepoys, 16
Sèvres, Treaty of, 20
Sharpe, Jenny, 41
Sherwood, Marcella, 19, 52
Shonfield, Andrew, 37
Showalter, Elaine, 104
Shusterman, David, 37–38
Shuttleworth, 107–8
Silver, Brenda, 41
Singh, Frances, 54
Sitwell, Constance, 87, 104
Song, 24, 68–69, 74, 86–87, 89
Spear, Percival, 14
Stallybrass, Oliver, 40
Stape, J. H., 40
Steel, Flora Annie, 53, 122
Stone, Wilfred, 38, 57–58
"The Story of a Panic," 91
Strachey, Lytton, 5, 8
Structure of the novel, 38, 57–58, 59, 61, 68, 89, 113–14, 117
Summers, Claude, 40
the Supernatural, 32, 62–63, 127, 131, 133, 134
Swaraj, 18, 56

The Tempest, 132
Thompson, George, 38
"Three Countries," 58
Tindall, W. Y., 37
Title of *A Passage to India*, 59–60
Traversi, Derek, 36
Trilling, Lionel, 36, 38, 68
Turkey, 20
Two Cheers for Democracy, 37

Upadhye, A. N., 98
Urdu, 11, 50, 84

Warren, Austin, 36
Wells, H. G., 4, 6
West, Rebecca, 35
Where Angels Fear to Tread, 20
Whitman, Walt, 59–60
Wilde, Alan, 39, 126
Wilde, Oscar, 7–8
Woolf, Leonard, 26, 28
Woolf, Virginia, 4–5, 6, 8, 32, 37
World War I, 8–9, 25
World War II, 13, 34, 124
Wurgaft, Lewis, 17, 41

The Author

Judith Scherer Herz is Professor of English at Concordia University in Montreal. She received her Ph.D. from the University of Rochester and has taught at Cornell University. She is the author of *The Short Narratives of E. M. Forster* (1988), coeditor of *E. M. Forster: Centenary Revaluations* (1982), and the author of articles on Forster, Chaucer, and Shakespeare as well as on Milton, Donne, and other seventeenth-century poets. She is past president of the Association of Canadian College and University Teachers of English (ACCUTE).